Intrepid
Arabia

William Dalrymple
Elliot Daniel
Peter Carty
Juliet Coombe
Matt Rudd
Nicholas Fogg
Sejal Mandalia
Amar Grover
Chris Doyle
Ed Waller
Penny Young
Mike Gerrard
Maria Golia
Tom Perry
Chris Bradley
Steve Davey

Edited by: Ian Jackson & Tom Tugendhat

La Belle Aurore

First published in Great Britain in 1999 by
La Belle Aurore
15 Ballater Road
London SW2 5QS
Tel: 0171–924 0856

Intrepid Arabia © La Belle Aurore 1999

ISBN 0 9534423 1 4

Editors: Ian Jackson & Tom Tugendhat

Concept and Finance: La Belle Aurore

Design and Production: Steve Davey, La Belle Aurore

Administration: Sejal Mandalia

Cover photography: Juliet Coombe, La Belle Aurore

Commmssioning Board:
Jon Leyne (BBC Journalist)
Claire Moody (Out of the Blue)
Sara Abuzaid (Council of Arab-British Understanding)

Printed by: Chromo Litho (01244–347544)

Contents

The Writers 4

Map of the Region 10

Foreward *Simon Calder* 11

Introduction *Marty Garret* 13

Palestine: The Monk's Tale *William Dalrymple* 15

Yemen: Branding Away the Demons *Elliot Daniel* 25

Iran: A Tale of Two Irans *Peter Carty* 35

Egypt: Cursed in the City of the Dead *Juliet Coombe* 45

Syria: On The Road To Damascus *Matt Rudd* 55

Jordan: Life, Love and War: A First Journey *Nicholas Fogg* 65

Palestine: From Debka to Break Dancing *Sejal Mandalia* 75

Morocco: The Last Resort *Amar Grover* 85

Israel: The Bedouin of the Negev *Chris Doyle* 95

Saudi Arabia: A Saudi Journey *Ed Waller* 105

Syria: On the Banks of the Euphrates *Penny Young* 115

Egypt: Life and Death on the Nile *Mike Gerrard* 125

Oman: Aromatic Oman *Maria Golia* 135

Lebanon: Easter in the Lebanon *Tom Perry* 145

Yemen: Walking the Valley of Death *Chris Bradley* 155

Turkey: Escape From Butterfly Valley *Steve Davey* 165

Countries of
Intrepid Arabia

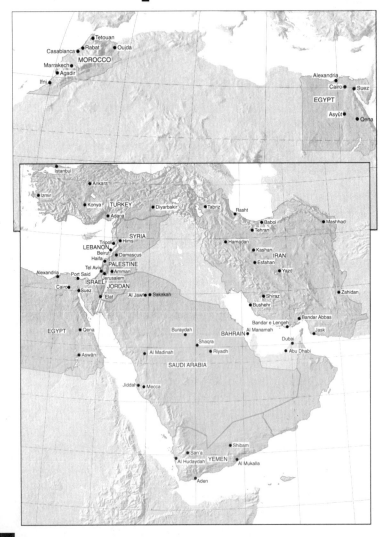

The Writers & Editors

Intrepid Arabia is the collaboration of a number of writers and editors from around the world.

Ian Jackson

En route to London, Ian Jackson spent 18 months in South East Asia. He got intimately acquainted with squat bogs in China, Vietnam, Thailand, Laos, Malaysia and Indonesia and travelled by boat, bus, train, horse, motorbike, truck, foot and countless other bizzare forms of transport. On his arrival in London he became travel editor and later editor of TNT Magazine, a leading publication for travellers and Australasians in the UK.

Tom Tugendhat

Tom has recently returned from two years in Beirut where he was writing for newspapers and magazines around the world. On a trip many years ago he fell for the Arab world and went on to learn more about the culture, culminating in a trip to Yemen while studying for an MPhil in Arab History and Language from Cambridge. He has visited much of the Middle East, but never quite got over his visit to Yemen, the heart of Arabia, the mountains around Sanaa.

William Dalrymple

William Dalrymple published the first in his series of highly acclaimed bestsellers, *In Xanadu*, at the tender age of twenty-two. His fourth book, *The Age of Kali* was published last year. William was recently elected the youngest Fellow of the Royal Society of Literature. He has written and presented a television programme on the architecture of the Raj for Channel 4 and has just completed Indian Journeys, a major series on the religions of India for BBC2.

Elliot Daniel

Journalist and filmaker, Elliot's work has appeared all round the world. He speaks regularly at conferences and at the Independent Travel World in London he showed his film *Demons in the Village* on the impact of global travel. He has an honours degree in Tourism and is currently researching its effects on hilltribe communities across Southeast Asia for his PhD. Elliot hopes that his stories will in some small way make our earth a kinder place.

Peter Carty

Peter is travel editor on Time Out magazine and contributes regularly to The Guardian. His travel experiences include trying to challenge a New York mugger to a game of Russian roulette, teaching quadratic equations to African township children, ingesting a hallucinogenic jungle vine with a Brazilian religious rainforest cult, and getting drunk in a castle outside Vienna with an Austrian artist who paints in blood and stages mass orgies.

Juliet Coombe

Juliet, co-founder of La Belle Aurore, began her career at the age of 17 as a photojournalist. A blind date with a tiger in Quito, witnessing an Indian blood sacrifice in Mexico, motorbiking along Cambodias Killer Highway and student riots in Burma are just some of the mishaps Juliet has had as a travel writer and photographer. Her stories have appeared in Time Out, Wanderlust magazine, Lonely Planet, and TNT magazine.

Matt Rudd

Matt Rudd has had itchy feet and a desire to write ever since he poisoned himself with a Zimbabwean biro at the age of two. After six months with Condé Nast Traveller, Matt joined Wanderlust magazine where he is now the Assistant Editor. This year's assignments have included nowhere warm: New England, Iceland, Lithuania and Kaliningrad, with recent contributions to Condé Nast Traveller and the Observer.

Nicholas Fogg

In his varied career, Nick has worked with International Aid agencies and as Media and Policy consultant to the Middle East Institute at Harvard. His published work includes, *Portraits of a Town*, *Brunels Flagship of the Steam Revolution*, and *Merrymaking and Frolic*. He has just completed a novel *A Trace of Shadow*. He has written for The Times, The Sunday Times, The Daily Telegraph, Evening Standard and the specialist press.

Sejal Mandalia

Sejal worked in Mumbai (Bombay) for India's biggest evening newspaper, Mid-Day. In between she managed to find time to do some stringing for The Sunday Times in London and The Khaleej Times in Dubai. Back in London, she has written Parliamentary briefs for the Council of Arab-British Understanding. She has also free-lanced with The Sunday Business, reporting on the Palestinian Authority.

Amar Grover

Born in Hong Kong of Indo-Irish parents, Amar decided to leave a two-year spell as a London solicitor and pursue his real interests – travel and photography. "I preferred meeting people to business meetings and journalism over jurisprudence," he says. Amar has contributed travel features to a variety of newspapers and magazines, including the Sunday Telegraph, Financial Times, Independent and Geographical Magazine.

Chris Doyle

Chris spent a year studying Arabic at Alexandria University. Then in 1993 he joined the Council for the Advancement of Arab-British Understanding (CAABU), where he is now Senior Information Officer. As a vegetarian, travelling in the Arab world has occasionally proved to be problematic for him and on a few occasions, he has had to eat meat in order not to offend his hosts. Eating a sheep's eyeball was a particular highlight.

Ed Waller

Ed escaped from a life of trade journalism when a two week holiday to Turkey turned into a two year trip around the East. Savoured memories include puppy-smuggling on the Trans-Mongolian Express, and the Nepalese anti-royalist riots of 1994. Previous employment includes cement mixing, politics teacher, trout farmer, nude model and working in an Israeli chocolate factory – obviously putting an MA in Philosophy to excellent use.

Penny Young

Penny gave up her job as news editor with BBC Radio Northampton, bought a bicycle and peddled off towards Istanbul. Her travels can be heard on BBC World Service, BBC Radio Four, Radio Deutsche Welle and Radio Netherlands. Her worst moments were being mistaken for an Israeli spy by Hezbollah in Southern Lebanon and being detained by Syrian police for taking a photo of a street in Damascus where President Assad lives.

Mike Gerrard

Mike began his travel writing career by going on a package holiday to Greece and sending an article to The Daily Telegraph. From reckless beginnings he has gone on to visit Siberia, go jungle-trekking in Sumatra, walk 100 miles in the Great Rift Valley in Tanzania and survive a weekend in Walsall. He writes mostly for Time Out, Wanderlust, The Times and The Independent on Sunday and has won a Travelex Award for his travel writing.

Maria Golia

A woman who regards cities as lovers, Maria Golia resided in Buenos Aires and the Cote d'Azur. Bombay, Kathmandu, Moscow, Dar es Salam and Muscat are a few of her other d'alliances, but no capital captured her attentions as completely as Cairo, where she has lived for over twelve years. Columnist for the Cairo Times, she has published in Egypt Today, the Middle East Times and the Al Ahram Weekly, the Middle East International and Fodors Guide to Egypt.

Tom Perry

Tom is currently a student of Arabic and Middle East History at the University of Manchester. He explored the Levant in 1997, travelling through Jordan, Egypt and Lebanon. He has written about his travels for the student press. Last year he taught in a refugee camp in Palestine. His scariest moment was when he found himself caught in a curfew in Hebron. The human rights observers requested his photo as a souvenir.

Chris Bradley

Chris spent eight years as a Tour Group leader in Egypt, Jordan, India and Central Asia. He still leads special interest groups. He has written for the Insight Yemen guide, as well as his own Discovery Guide. As a filmmaker, he wrote and produced a documentary on the Shetland Oil Disaster for National Geographic. He lectures at the Royal Geographical Society and contributes to Wanderlust, Trail Walker, Arabian Wildlife and Mountain Biking UK.

Steve Davey

Believing that life can sometimes be too normal and safe, Steve has combed the world in the constant search for that rush of excitement, following the theory that if you aren't in the middle of the action – whether as a photographer and writer, or just in life – then you might just as well pack up and go home. Home is Brixton in London – the closest you can get to travelling without needing your passport – in an eclectic house dominated by a rather large cat.

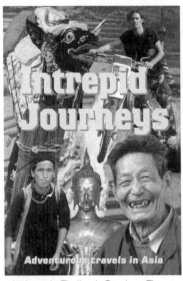

Adventurous travels in Asia

Want more Intrepid Tales?

Free Postage in the UK

This is your chance to send off for a copy of our first collection: Intrepid Journeys, sixteen inspiring stories from Asia.

Intrepid Journeys can be difficult or arduous, but always have a positive or uplifting resolution – the very essence of travel.

Included in the book are Wanderlust Editor, Lyn Hughes' travels on an elephant in Thailand; Sundays Times writer, Mark Hodson's bus ride in the Philippines; TNT Magazine Editor, Ian Jackson's motorbike ride through Vietnam and Josie Dew's encounter with a typhoon in Japan.

Intrepid Journeys has been featured in the London Evening Standard, The Guardian, Southern Cross, Cycling Magazine, The Independent, Wanderlust Magazine, Time Out Magazine, TNT Magazine, the Daily Mail and the Australian Herald Sun.

Intrepid Journeys is the ideal entertainment for the armchair traveller and the perfect companion for those on Intrepid Journeys of their own.

Intrepid Journeys is available for just £4.99 with free postage and packing in the UK only

For Europe, please add £1.00
Rest of the world, please add £1.75

Cheques, postal orders or bankers drafts in Sterling only please, made payable to Intrepid Journeys:

La Belle Aurore Book Orders
28 Calvin Street, London E1 6NW.

For more information or bulk discounts:

Tel: +44 207 – 247 5351
Fax: +44 207 – 377 9486
E-mail: orders@aurore2.demon.co.uk

Orders normally dispatched within five working days.

For a limited time you can also order extra copies of Intrepid Arabia at £4.99 with free postage and packing in the UK only!

Foreward

Your first experience of Arabia may be like mine: a dazzling confusion of old and new; tradition co-existing with modernity in a headlong rush towards the 21st Century, without neglecting Arab customs of travel and trade in a spirit of hospitality and generosity. And that was just the duty-free shop at Dubai airport.

For far too many people, that is as close as they get to Arabia. If this splendid collection of travellers' tales serves simply to inspire others to visit the area that we in the West describe as the Near and Middle East, it will have been worthwhile.

On a purely touristic level, Maria Golia's spirited account of Oman had me checking the flight schedules there, while Tom Perry's entrancing tale of Easter in Lebanon demanded a more complex itinerary. If I ever need to dispel a demon or two, I shall follow Elliot Daniel's journey to Nafha, the revered witch of Yemen.

The central theme throughout this book is of increasing understanding. Say "Agadir" to most tourists, and they will immediately think of the Moroccan resort of that name. Amar Grover's exploration of the *agadir* — fortress granary — in Amtoudi, Morocco, expands our view of the world way beyond the brochures. But that we travellers are not, as a breed, fully evolved to deal with the supposed rigours of life east of Istanbul is demonstrated by Steve Davey's hilarious account of the *nadir* of backpacker culture. More encouraging is Ed Waller's exploration of Saudi Arabia, where Western tourism is as yet embryonic.

The writers here overturn a preconception or three; Peter Carty's fears that Iran may live up to the image popular in the West that it is a nation with "a fundamental abhorrence of outsiders" proves entirely unfounded. Mike Gerrard examines the concept of *baksheesh* and our misunderstandings of it. Penny Young recommends political leaders follow her on the road to Damascus to "consider the civilisations that have risen and fallen" alongside the murky waters of the Euphrates.

While most pages of this book reverberate with life, there is a respect for death: Juliet Coombe's shocking account of how the two converge at cemeteries in Cairo, and Chris Bradley's epic journey into Yemen's 'Valley of Death'. The master storyteller William Dalrymple brings to life the 'River of Blood' and the 'Valley of Doom'.

Nicholas Fogg's haunting account of Jordan in 1970 reflects the tension in the region that bring new tragedy all too often. It is followed by Sejal Mandalia's celebration of life in the Gaza Strip; and vegetarian Chris Doyle's confrontation with dead flesh with the Bedouin of the Negev, whose traditions know no frontier yet whose future lies in the cauldron of conflict between Israel and its neighbours.

Matt Rudd recounts the observation of a Dutch diplomat in Beirut: "Spend a day in Lebanon and you could write a book. Spend a week and you could only write a chapter. Spend a year and you won't be able to write a word". Between them, the contributors have spent many decades in Arabia, and thankfully they have collaborated on a classic. May it take you to Dubai duty-free shop and beyond in a spirit of adventure — and respect.

Simon Calder
Travel editor of The Independent and presenter for BBC-2's Travel Show.

Introduction

We all yearn for exotic lands and a chance to live in them but rarely get the opportunity, save for a brief vacation. My vacation has lasted ten years and continues to this day.

And it's been a very unusual ten years since I arrived in Cairo. Working as a Tour Leader was a great insight into the people who travel on an adventure tour and an opportunity next to none to experience a country and it's people first hand. Since settling down in Egypt to run the Imaginative Traveller Middle East operation, there has never been a day that I don't look at the Pyramids from my living-room window and pause for just a moment.

I find it hard to put into words just what Cairo is all about, the amazing traffic (yet never a traffic jam!), the noise and excitement of a Thursday evening, when the millions pour into the city for their weekend break. The Friday silence as the city sleeps then awakens for midday prayers. Though exciting, Egypt's capital city seems a world apart from the rest of this fascinating land. Aswan is a breath of fresh air and my favourite escape. Here golden sand dunes tumble to the edge of the river Nile and graceful sailboats glide around the islands. The city itself is constantly enchanting and seems to be immune to change, so strong is its Nubian culture.

Israel is just a coach trip away yet the contrast is amazing. The vibrant streets and beachfront of Tel Aviv, so reminiscent of Mediterranean Europe, seem almost out of place. Yet just an hour away is Jerusalem. Dodging the handcarts and hawkers as I walk though the narrow alleyways and passages of the old walled city, it's impossible not to dwell on the fact that for centuries this city has been at the centre of our history.

It is contrasts like these that make the Middle East such a stimulating place to live. Despite constant invasions from travellers and adventurers for so many years, and with so many modern influences pressuring to get in, it has retained its dignity and its character.

Many countries in the region are still coming to terms with the modern world, a world where global communications make it extremely hard to keep nations in the dark, but in many regards, it is right that people should cherish the 'old ways'.

They have kept their respect for elders and their commitment to family. The region boasts few old folks homes and less homeless than any Western country.

It may sound incredible to someone who hasn't been here, especially when so many high profile conflicts have taken place in this corner of the world, but the streets of Cairo and Amman are some of the safest I know.

Forget the news, there isn't a part of the world where you will receive a warmer or more genuine welcome.

Marty Garrett
Regional Manager Middle East
The Imaginative Traveller

The Monk's Tale

by William Dalrymple

"Look at it," said Fr. Theophanes waving a hand at the dark rocky gorge beneath us. "There it is: the 'Valley of Doom'. 'The Valley of Dreadful Judgement'."

Below us the monastic buildings of Mar Saba fell away in a ripple of chapels, cells and oratories, each successive layer hanging like a swallow's nest from a ledge on the rockface. Opposite, the top of the cliff wall had turned an almost unnatural shade of red in the evening light. The rock was pitted with a honeycomb of caves, each formerly the cell of a Byzantine monk. All were now deserted.

"It's very beautiful," I said.

"Beautiful," said Fr. Theophanes, rustling his robes in horror. "Beautiful. See down there at the bottom? The river. Nowadays it's just the sewage from Jerusalem. But on Judgement Day that's where the River of Blood is going to flow. It's going to be full of freemasons, whores and heretics. Protestants, Schismatics, Jews, Catholics. More *Ouzo*?"

"Please."

The monk paused to pour another thimbleful of spirit into a small glass. When I had gulped it down, he continued with his apocalypse:

"At the head of the Damned will be a troop composed of all the Popes of Rome, followed by their deputies, the Vice-Presidents of the Freemasons."

"You're saying the Pope is a Freemason?"

"A Freemason? He's the President of the Freemasons. Everyone knows this. Each morning he worships the devil in the form of a naked woman with the head of a goat."

"Actually, I'm a Catholic."

"Then," said Fr. Theophanes, "unless you convert to Orthodoxy, you will follow your Pope down that valley, through the scorching fire. We will watch you from this balcony," he added. "But of course it will then be too late to save you."

I smiled, but Fr. Theophanes was in full swing and in no mood for joking.

"No one can truly know what that day will be like," he said shaking his gravely.

"But some of our Orthodox Fathers have had visions. Fire — fire that will never end, terrible, terrible fire, will come from the throne of Christ, just like it is on the icons. The saints — those who are to be saved, in other words the Orthodox Church — will fly in the air to meet Christ. But sinners and all non-Orthodox will be separated from the Elect. The damned will be pushed and prodded by devils down through the fire, down from the Valley of Josephat, past here — in fact exactly the route those Israeli hikers took today — down, down to the 'Mouth of Hell.'"

"Is that nearby?"

"Certainly," said Fr. Theophanes, stroking his beard. "The 'Mouth of Hell' will open up near the Dead Sea."

"That is in the Bible?"

"Of course. Everything I am telling you is true," said Fr. Theophanes.

"Look at those clouds in the east," said Fr. Evdokimos, the deputy *archimandrite* (abbot), deliberately changing the subject. "There may be rain tomorrow. What do you think, Theophanes?"

"The rains here in Palestine are not like the rains of Greece," replied the other monk. "There we get big rains, proper cloudbursts."

Fr. Theophanes smiled happily at the memory: "Ah, the rains of Greece," he said. "They are a reminder of 'The Deluge'."

I had arrived at the Great Lavra of Mar Saba earlier that afternoon. The monastery lies 15 miles from Jerusalem, a little to the north of the Dead

Sea. Above Bethlehem, where you first enter the West Bank, the soil is still fertile and the olive trees stand out against terraces cut into the hard white hillsides. But as you drive on, the cultivation recedes. The soil becomes thinner, the valleys deeper, and the villages poorer. The driver warned that we were entering *Hamas* territory and hung a Palestinian *keffiyeh* (checked scarf) over half the windscreen to make sure we would not be mistaken for Israeli settlers and stoned by the local *shabab.*

Passing the last village, we entered the desert. Below us the barren shale hills fell away towards the lowest point on earth, the Dead Sea, a quivering drop of mercury in the distance. Straight ahead, a pair of small rectangular Byzantine watchtowers rose vertically against the lip of a deep wadi. In the 40 miles of landscape visible from the hilltop, those two towers were the only buildings in sight.

It was only when you passed underneath the machicolation of the nearest tower that you caught your first glimpse of the monastery that lay hidden in the depth of the gorge. The two towers were linked by a great wall which swept downwards in a U-shaped bend to enclose turquoise domes and copulas, balconies and cave-cells, all propped up by great lines of massive, heavy buttresses.

In the middle of the sixth century AD the wastes of Judea had become so filled with monks and monasteries that, according to one chronicler, "the desert had become a city". Yet of the 150-odd monastic settlements founded during the Byzantine rule, only six are still occupied. Of those only one, Mar Saba, still supports enough monks to really qualify as a living monastery. It has been occupied continuously since its foundation in the late fifth century, except for a two-week hiatus following the massacre of the monks by marauding Persians in 613 AD. The divine office has been sung in the rock chapel of St. Sabas every morning for the last 1517 years. The skulls of the hundreds of monks killed by the Persians, along with those subsequently murdered by marauding Bedouin, have been carefully kept in the abbey church, stacked in neat rows as nonchalantly as other churches might stack their hymn books.

Mar Saba remains one of the most austere of monasteries. The monks rise at two in the morning and sing the office for five hours, until dawn begins to break over the iconostasis of the abbey church. The fathers then rest until eleven when they eat their one meal of the day: bread (baked once a week, nice enough for three days but increasingly stale and mouldy thereafter), thin soup, boiled vegetables and strong Greek cheese. They do not eat meat, while fish and oil (for dressing the vegetables) are only allowed on Sundays and feast days. After their meal they retire to their caves and cells for the rest of the day, emerging only to sing lauds, vespers and compline at the appointed times.

If Mar Saba is now mainly remarkable for the terrible severity of its asceticism, it was once famous for its scholarship. When the English pilgrim St. Willibald visited the monastery in the early eighth century the monks were busy copying manuscripts and composing some of the most beautiful hymns and poems ever written in Byzantium. But you would never guess any of this from talking to Mar Saba's current inhabitants,

"So you're a writer are you?" asked Fr. Theophanes when he brought me my supper on a tray at the end of vespers. "I've stopped reading books myself. 'The Divine Liturgy' contains all the theology I need. Once you've read the word of God I can't see the point of reading anything else."

"They say books are like food," pointed out Fr. Evdokimos, philosophically. "They feed your brain."

"But Father," said Fr. Theophanes quietly. "Monks should try to eat as little as possible."

It was nearly dark. As we talked, Fr. Theophanes took out a box of matches and began to try and light a pair of battered old paraffin storm lanterns (there is no electricity in Mar Saba).

"What did you do before you became a monk?" I asked as Fr. Theophanes sat trimming the wicks.

"I was a policeman in Athens. I came here for the first time on a pilgrimage. As soon as I saw this monastery I recognised it as my true home. I went back to Athens, gave in my resignation and said good-bye to my mother. A week later I was back here. Since then I've never left."

"Never?"

"I went back only once. For 40 days."

"Was that difficult?"

"My mother cried sometimes. But otherwise, no. Things change very quickly. I hardly recognised my old city. My people had suddenly become rich from your European Community. There were so many new buildings. New buildings and new crimes."

"It must all have been a quite a change from your previous work."

"Not so different," replied the monk. "Demons are very like criminals.

Both are very stupid. Both are damned."

The lanterns were alight now, casting shadows over the room and across the face of Fr. Theophanes.

"You don't actually believe in demons?" I asked.

"Of course. They are in the Bible."

"Sometimes when we are praying the demons make strange noises," added Fr. Evdokimos, who had been sitting quietly in the corner, stroking his beard. "At first I thought it was just the animals of the desert. But then I noticed the noises came most loudly when I was praying. It is the demons trying to distract us."

"Each demon has its own personality," added Fr. Theophanes. "They live in the desert and come to the cities to make men into criminals, Catholics and Freemasons."

"They can work miracles and make false prophecies," said Fr. Evdokimos.

"They are worse than criminals," said Fr. Theophanes. "But here, within the walls of Mar Saba, we are protected."

"What do you mean?"

"St. Sabas is alive here. He protects his monastery. I have experienced it myself."

"How?" I asked.

"Three years ago on a windy night in the winter I was praying in my cave. It was night and I had not lit a lamp so my cell was pitch black. As I prayed I heard footsteps coming up the corridor. It was the noise of a monk walking: I could hear the rustling of his habit. The footsteps came closer and closer and then stopped outside my room. I waited for the monk to speak but nothing happened. Suddenly I heard very clearly the noise of hundreds of feet tripping down the stairs from the opposite direction. They were like madmen, jumping down the steps very quickly — loud, irregular footsteps. There were maybe five or six of them, all running. I thought: the Bedouin have climbed the walls and broken in and now they want to kill us. I froze behind my door, but nothing happened. After five minutes they still didn't come in. So very slowly I opened the door and went out," said Fr. Theophanes.

"It was a full moon that night. I could see clearly that the corridor was empty. There was silence in the monastery. I walked up to the courtyard and at that moment I saw Fr. Evdokimos' light moving from the latrines to his room. So I went up and said: 'Father — there are thieves in the monastery.' He asked: 'You are sure?' I said I was. 'Alright,' he said, 'we'll look together.' So we both took sticks and for an hour we went all around. We searched in the church, in the towers, inside the deepest caves. Nothing: the door was secure and no one had come in over the wall."

"It was only later," said Fr. Evdokimos taking up the tale, "when we discussed the matter with the abbot that we understood what had happened. The first set of footsteps were those of St. Sabas. The loud rabble were demons coming to turn Fr. Theophanes into a Freemason. St. Sabas knew what they were planning so he stood in front of Fr. Theophanes' door to guard it. Then he chased the demons away."

"The devil will capture everyone if he gets the chance," said Fr. Theophanes gravely. "But the saints protect us. In this monastery I feel secure, although it is in the middle of the desert, with Bedouin all around us. We are protected."

It was late and the monks began to drift off to their cells carrying their lanterns. Fr. Theophanes showed me to my cell and promised to come and wake me for matins at 2am.

All night, it seemed, bells were peeling. At 1am a monk began to knock the wooden *simandron* to call the brethren from their beds; he rang it again at 1.30am and at 1.55am. At 2am I was treated to a full scale bell-ringing performance: the bells in the campanile supplemented by a selection of handbells, one rung very loudly at the door of my cell by Fr. Theophanes. But as soon as silence had returned I fell asleep again and it was nearly 4am before I finally pulled myself out of bed. It was pitch dark and very cold. I dressed by the light of the lantern then picked my way downstairs through the empty stairways and corridors of Mar Saba, towards the deep swell and eddy of monastic chant.

In the church all the lamps were lit, casting a dim glow over the basilica. The monastic kyries echoed around the dome. Only the occasional creek of a misericord gave away the position of the singers, the monks themselves were invisible in their black robes as they roosted in the choirstalls. Every so often a breeze would swing one of the chandeliers, rotating it slightly so that shadows raced around the church, the returning flash of candlelight picking out the highlights in the frescoes: the wings of angels and the long white beards of the desert fathers. The chant eddied out across the narrow valley, echoed and amplified by the domes and copulas.

Towards 6am first light began to filter in, gently illuminating the Christ Pantocrator in the dome. Half-an-hour later, with the sun rising over the desert, you could pick out the monks themselves, black-bearded, black-robed, hooded and cowled in their stalls. What I initially took to be a low table near the lectern turned out to be Fr. Evdokimos kneeling, bent forward on the ground in a long prostration before the iconostasis.

One by one the monks glided from the church, each stopping to kiss the most sacred icons as they went. An hour later I returned to my bed, and slept until noon when Fr. Theophanes brought me my lunch on a tray and announced that the van would soon be ready to carry me to Jerusalem. He stood by as I ate, like a *maitre d'hote* waiting to see a patron's reaction to some especially delicate *soufflé*. This precipitated something of an etiquette problem.

Lunch at Mar Saba was never a very ritzy affair at the best of times, but towards the end of the week, when the bread baked days earlier had hardened to the texture of pumice, and when the feta cheese had begun to smell increasingly like dead goat, eating Fr. Theophanes's offerings became something of a penitential exercise and sounding sincere in one's appreciation of the monks' culinary abilities was a task that needed advanced acting skills. I looked at the lump of rock-bread and the festering goat's cheese, and tried to think of something nice to say about them. Then I had a flash of inspiration:

"Mmm," I said, taking a sip from the glass. "Delicious water, Fr. Theophanes."

This, oddly enough, went down very well.

"The water here is very sweet." The monk allowed himself a brief smile.

"Very sweet, Fr. Theophanes."

"During this summer we had a drought," continued Fr. Theophanes. "Our cisterns were beginning to run dry. August went by. Then September. One after another our cisterns gave up. We were like the Children of Israel in the wilderness. But St. Sabas takes care of us. We are never without some drinking water. We always have the spring."

"The spring?"

"The spring of St. Sabas. He prayed and it came. You do not know the story?"

"Tell it to me."

"In the days of St. Sabas more and more monks were joining the lavra to be with the saint. Eventually the number of brethren grew to 700 and there was no more water to go around. So St. Sabas prayed. For 30 days and 30 nights he prayed on the roof of his cell, refusing to eat in the hope that our Lord would look down with mercy on his people. Finally, at the end of the 30 days and 30 nights, it happened to be a full moon. St. Sabas went onto the roof for the last time to beg the Lord for mercy. He began to pray when all of a sudden he heard the beating of a wild ass's hooves in the valley below. He looked out and saw the animal. It was charging down the valley as if sent by the Angel Gabriel himself. Then it stopped, looked around and began digging deep into the gravel. It dug for 20 minutes then it bent down and began to drink.

"St. Sabas spent the night giving thanks to the Lord. The following morning he climbed down the cliffs. At the bottom, just as he expected, he found that the ass had revealed a spring of living water at the foot of the cliffs. It was a constant supply that never ever fails. Even today. Incidentally it tastes very good in *Ouzo*. All this is one of the compensations that St. Sabas gives us for our sufferings."

"What are the others?" I asked.

"There are many," he said. "But the most remarkable is this — after we leave our mortal frame, our bodies never grow stiff."

"I'm sorry?"

"After we are dead we never get stiff. We never suffer from ... how do you say..."

"Corruption? Decomposition?"

"That's right, decomposition." Fr. Theophanes rolled the words around his mouth as if savouring the notion of mortal decay. "But with the monks of this monastery, instead of giving off a foul stench of decay we emit a sweet fragrance. Like the scent of precious myrrh."

I must have looked sceptical for Fr. Theophanes added: "It is true," he said. "Many scientists have visited the monastery and declared themselves baffled. Anyway," he said, changing the subject, "I've just had a strange visitor at the monastery gate. It was a Bedouin. They are always looking for buried gold and sometimes they ring the bell of the monastery and ask for incense from the cave of St. Sabas to help them find what they are looking for."

"How does the incense help?"

"Sometimes they find gold in caves or old ruins, but they dare not take it in case it is guarded by a *djinn* (evil spirit). They go to their *Sheiks*, but they can do nothing so the *Sheiks* tell them to come here. The Muslims believe that if they get incense from here they can burn it and the holy fumes will scare away the *djinn*."

"Do you give them incense?" I asked.

"No. It would be blasphemous to use a holy substance for such a purpose. But sometimes I wonder..."

"What do you mean?"

"Well, once a man from Bethlehem came here. He was a taxi driver, named Mohammed. I knew him a little because he sometimes brought monks or pilgrims to us. Anyway, one day he rang the bell and asked for incense saying that he had found some gold in a pot that had been turned up by a plough on the land belonging to his family. He said his family were worried in case it was guarded by an evil *djinn*. I said no, he could not have it. Now he is dead. Sometimes I wonder whether I should have said yes."

"What do you mean 'now he is dead'?"

"He left here, went home and broke open the pot. Straight away he went crazy. He got iller and iller, skinnier and skinnier. Before he was a strong man. But slowly he became like a skeleton. Bones, a little skin, nothing more. Finally, three months ago, he died."

Fr. Theophanes shook his head: "The Muslims think the djinns are different from demons, but this is just a trick of the devil. There is no such thing as djinns: just devils in disguise. Now this man's soul will go to Hell."

Fr. Theophanes crossed himself, from right to left in the Orthodox manner: "He lost the gold and he lost his soul. Now he will burn like a Freemason."

"Fr. Theophanes," I asked, my curiosity finally getting the better of me. "I don't understand why you are so worried by the Freemasons."

"Because they are the 'Legions of the Anti-Christ. The 'Storm-troopers of the Whore of Babylon'."

"I always thought Freemasons just held coffee mornings and whist drives , that sort of thing."

"Wheest drives?" said Fr. Theophanes, pronouncing the word as if it was some sort of Satanic ritual. "Probably this wheest drive also. But their main activity is to worship the Devil. There are many steps," he said, nodding knowingly. "But the last, the final step, is to meet with the Devil and have homosexual relations with him. After this he makes you Pope, or sometimes President of the United States."

"President of the United States?"

"Certainly. This has been proved. All the Presidents of the United States have been Freemasons. Except Kennedy, and you know what happened to him."

Fr. Theophanes was still raving about the Freemasons and the way they had masterminded the Ecumenical movement and invented the supermarket bar code when a young novice knocked on the door to say the van was ready to take me to Jerusalem. Fr. Theophanes helped carry my luggage to the gate.

"Be careful," he said, as we stood by the great blue door. "These are the 'Last Days'. They are near their goal. They are everywhere now. Always be on your guard."

"Good-bye Fr. Theophanes," I said. "Thank you for everything."

"They say this may be the last Pope."

"Yes?"

"Some Holy Fathers have said this. Then the Arabs will be in Rome and the 'Whore of Babylon' will be in the Vatican."

"And the Freemasons?"

"These people. Who knows what they will do," Fr. Theophanes frowned. "Anyway," he said, "you must visit us again."

"Thank you."

"Maybe you will have converted to Orthodoxy by then?"

I smiled.

"I will pray for you, while there is still time. Maybe you can be saved."

Taking a huge key from a gaoler's ring, the monk undid the multiple bolts of the low gate in the monastery wall. "Think about it seriously," said Fr. Theophanes as he let me out. "Remember you will be among the damned if you don't."

The heavy metal door swung closed behind me. Outside, a dust storm was beginning.

Branding Away the Demons

by Elliot Daniel

My vehicle was part of a military convoy following a road known as 'Kidnap Highway' which ran through northern Yemen to the town of Sada near the undefined border with Saudi Arabia. An open back truck armed with eight soldiers gripping automatic rifles led the way. A soldier manned a giant machine gun that was bolted to the back of the truck. He looked ready to explode into action at the slightest provocation.

I had come to the legendary home of the Queen of Sheba to track down the mystics of Yifrus. In Yemen the world of the supernatural is intertwined with everyday life. People wander the streets concealing sacred items for protection against evil. Women pay money to witches so they find the perfect husband and students pay for top exam results.

The route I was travelling was dangerous, but I was looking for a revered witch called Nafha. If I could find her, maybe she could help rid me of the ghosts that tormented my soul. We were stopped every 20 to 30 miles at military checkpoints. If you do not possess the appropriate paper work in this notorious region you are unceremoniously sent back to Sana'a, the new political capital of the United Yemen Arab Republic.

After eight long, sweaty hours I was dropped off in Sada. Searching for some relief from the hot, stale, sticky air, I crossed the road and bought some *foul*; a sizzling concoction of beans, tomatoes, garlic, onions and eggs. Rows of chickens turned slowly on an open spit as swirls of sand lightly covered the roasting birds with grit. Old men sipped cups of cinnamon tea and clutched their *jambias*, (large J-shaped daggers), recalling Sada's heyday as a Zaidi capital and Royalist stronghold. Their eyes were excited, their mouths stuffed with green, narcotic *qat* leaves gave the impression that they had swallowed a golf ball or suffered from chronic toothache.

Suddenly, as a cup of sweet tasting tea arrived, Sada erupted into an explosion of bullets, mortars and bombs which shook my wooden table so much my drink went everywhere. I could not understand why everyone was running towards the action. All around me people were whooping with joy and screaming *Al-hamdulilah*, "thanks be to God" as their vehicles plunged head-long into the gun fire. Another spray of bullets flashed across the sky sending me ducking for cover.

The night sky turned into a laser display of gun fire and I wondered whether Saudi Arabia or America had declared war on Yemen. The old men roared with laughter at the sight of me huddled beneath the table, clutching onto its leg for dear life. They chuckled so hard they almost fell off their stools and gasped helplessly as the huge balls of leaves got stuck in their throats.

"What's so bloody funny," I snarled under my breath, humiliated by my cowardly antics. I stood up, brushing sand and grit from my jeans and tried to assess the situation. Ezzy, my Yemeni travelling companion came to my rescue as I shakily reclaimed my cinnamon tea. He was an ex-Olympic athlete with short greying hair which gave him a distinguished air.

"Everything is OK," he said, genuinely attempting to hide his amusement. "The people are celebrating the return of their loved ones from the annual Muslim pilgrimage to Mecca. The gunfire is perfectly normal. It's like a party".

"Great," I exclaimed. "What do you guys do for a stag night?"

Before I arrived in Yemen the media was full of reports describing the country as a lawless and dangerous place where tribes of ruthless warriors ruled the country with Kalashnikov rifles and other heavy weapons. So as another spray of bullets arched its way over the old town, I tried to order a beer to steady my nerves, forgetting that buying and selling alcohol is a crime which can lead to life imprisonment in Yemen.

Back in my hotel room, my head reverberating from the crackle of gun fire, I slept fitfully. The sounds continued into the early hours, sending chills down my body and comfort to the souls of Sada whose loved ones had returned home safely. The brilliant sprays of shrapnel illuminated the sky with vivid reds, greens and yellows. I finally fell asleep at about 5am, only to see the colours of the tracer bullets transformed into the scales of a huge black snake rearing its menacing face above me.

I awoke shaking. Outside, it was dark and deathly quiet. I walked cautiously beneath the giant arches and through the stone wall gate of Bab Al Yemen into the old city. I felt as if I had entered another beautiful world. But for the people of Yemen, such beauty came at a price.

Until as recently as 1962, while the Western world enjoyed the benefits of electricity, cars, washing machines and dishwashers, the families of Yemen had nothing. Their ruler, Imam Ahmed, closed the country in an effort to shut out the modern world. The last Imam of Yemen, ruled over one of the world's longest running dynasties and his loyal subjects were forcibly shackled by ignorance and archaic traditions. Perhaps the most bitter-sweet discovery for the revolutionaries occurred when they invaded the Imam's palace in Taiz and the secrets of his double life were revealed. Here they found all the modern luxuries they had been denied. For years he was revered as Ahmed Ya Djinah, the Controller of Evil and employed modern technology to trick his subjects into believing he possessed extraordinary powers.

They discovered tape-recorders which he had secretly hidden in his palace to record conversations which were then played back to people, convincing them that Ahmed Ya Djinah could communicate with the spirits.

Sada's backstreets reflected the neglect of his tyrannical rule. Many houses were without electricity. The streets were silent and old men hunched over thick, gritty coffees. Several stopped me and asked:

"Where are you from?"

"Australia," I would reply.

"Welcome to Yemen." A tiny gesture, yet it felt extremely reassuring in a land where virtually every man brandishes a *jambia* on his belt and drapes a sub-machine gun over his shoulder.

The early morning call to prayer suddenly boomed from the minaret's loud speakers, piercing the stillness. Devout, bleary-eyed Muslims shuffled towards the great mosque. Hunched over, the men removed their shoes outside the entrance and with their soles facing they disappeared into the darkness together. I yearned to follow , but sadly non-Muslims cannot go inside the Mosque's inner sanctum in Yemen. The guide books and locals, however, told me foreigners could enter the mosque at Yifrus where my journey would soon take me.

Nearby, amidst a selection of tools sat an ageing, ebony skinned man, his fingers covered in grease. A gas bottle spurted a flame on top of his tiny anvil. This was one of the 'fix-it-men'. People brought anything and everything to him to be repaired. I stared in amazement as he ingeniously solved the community's household problems. I wondered where he had come from and what his background was. Rigid class structures still exist in Yemen and ones choice of job and potential partner are decided by family and tribal elders. I left him as a little kid tugged at his sleeve, clutching a broken pedal from his bike.

I rarely saw women inside the dark and mysterious old city. When I did, they were covered from head to toe, in dresses, cloths, shawls and veils, many of them black. Such modesty is demanded by strict Islam law. I was mesmerised by one woman, a black crow, scurrying through narrow alleyways dragging kids with each arm behind her. Outside her home she pulled a giant wooden key, in the shape of a toothbrush with pegs from her dress and used it to open a medieval lock before disappearing behind the stone fortress.

It was still mid-morning and not too hot, so Ezzy and I left the Imam's ancient fiefdom and set off for *suq* Al Talh, roughly 12 kilometres outside Sada. This 'gun market' has the reputation of being the focus of illegally smuggled goods from Saudi Arabia. You name it, this market has it. There were rows and rows of shipping containers full of weapons. You could buy everything, from unlimited green and yellow packing cases full of bullets to pistols, rifles and machine guns.

"How much for this one?" I asked one of the gun merchants. A Russian Kalashnikov cost US$200 and an Israeli assault rifle, US$100. But he was more eager to show me his impressive pen-gun collection. On the outside the pens looked exactly the same as those used in an office, but with a flick they became lethal weapons. Ezzy said they were essential for getting a pay rise. Next to these sat grenades, bombs, and rockets — enough of an arsenal to start World War III.

Everywhere I looked people were stocking up on bullets and discussing the festival which would occur the following day. Each year all the men in the district converge upon 'moon mountain', a sacred spot outside Sada to celebrate the returnees from Mecca. I decided to join them on the trucks that hurtled across bone-crunching roads, spewing dust everywhere.

As we approached the sacred mountain, the sound of gun fire increased. From the relative safety of a few hundred metres away, I observed a sea of men wearing turbans, all of them heavily armed, dancing, singing, playing drums and rejoicing whilst firing machine guns into the air, into cliffs, in fact anywhere they wanted. Waves of trucks and columns of men walking in unison appeared on the horizon like an army of red, black and white ants. At the front of each group was a huge banner brandishing the tribes' name and affiliations. It was a flexing of tribal muscles, where powerful men rejoiced and strutted amid the shells of destruction. I stood watching. Vulnerable. Breathless. The deafening explosion of a bomb shook the ground under me and echoed through my head.

Hours later I could still hear the noise of ammunition several miles into my journey as the northern frontier of Sada faded into a whirlwind of dust and mixed emotions. Through the vehicle window was a land of 1001 mirages. Giant volcanic mountains, spat out by the earth, now run like arteries through the heart of Yemen. Nearby lay the Rub Al Khali, the wild and lawless desert region which covers most of the Arabian Peninsula. I was bound for Yifrus, a centre of mysticism and occult healing for more than 1500 years. Here, through divine intervention, believers' evils are exorcised.

For many, the gleaming white mosque of Yifrus means an end to their search. This 16th century mosque was dedicated to a venerated religious man, Ibn Alwan. The mosque's minarets glistened, a shining beacon against the rugged mountain backdrop. People pay homage at his shrine and asked to be blessed and relieved from their demons and ailments. I had travelled to this mosque because I saw it as a fascinating window into the lives of the Yemeni people.

I climbed the staircase and entered the mosque's inner courtyard. Attempting to cross the threshold of the main door I was firmly stopped by the watchman. I stood dumbfounded. I had come all this way to enter the world of mystics, yet was being denied entry. The Koran, as far as I knew, says that non-Muslims cannot visit the holy site of Mecca; it doesn't say anything about other temples. But the watchman would have none of it. I didn't know what to do, so I sat on the cold stone steps where I began to ask questions to the men gathered around me.

A man dressed in a long white *futah* and wearing a white cap and white beard was introduced as the reigning Imam. He said he had been the mosque's religious ruler for 25 years. The act of self-flagellation was definitely practised here, he told me, and in case his word was not enough he called to a short, stocky man who obediently stabbed himself with a knife, his pupils rolling back and leaving only the haunting whites of his eyes visible.

This man's illness was *djinn* (evil), and to rid himself of it he tore open his shirt and began slashing his *jambia* knife across the lower left part of his stomach. A dark brown scar lay where the blade had pierced his skin again and again, but not one slash left a new mark. I noticed his eyes were fiery and glazed from chewing *qat* leaves.

Until recently chewing *qat* was reserved for mystics and religious men who used it to get closer to their God. Today, everyone chews it, regardless of age or gender. *Qat*'s addiction is said to be reminiscent of love — "it can be the gift of heavenly happiness, but also the knife of weakness driven into your guts".

Both the Imam and Ezzy, who was born into one of the most sacred families of the prophet Mohammed, the Al Radha family or Mubarak people, tolerated this man's rituals yet sceptically dismissed them as "no good". Such actions were steeped in superstition, founded on myths and the supernatural and not based on the healing powers of the Koran.

Shocked, I returned to the car and went in search of Nafha, a woman I had heard about after talking with journalists from the Yemen Times newspaper. A powerful desire to enter the spiritual world of Yemen burned deep inside me. My entire body trembled with excitement. Lurking in the depths of my being lay personal demons that continued to torment me and I yearned for an end to my nightmares. Nafha was one of the most respected and revered healers in the country. She held the key to exorcising my demons.

My quest had begun years earlier and thousands of miles away in Northern Thailand. I had been swimming in a river in the hills and as the current carried me downstream I felt the hand of an unseen spirit pulling me down. It was the closest I had come to drowning and the nearest I had been to death. That fear clung to me and guided me to a local witch doctor who told me of the spirit. He was the river god, a snake who would test me three times. Only the third test remained and I wondered when he would strike next. The fear haunted me and I knew only Nafha could release me.

Her three-story mud brick home lay about 90 minutes drive from Yifrus at the village of Al Maseeria in the Shah Oba region. It lay in an ancient wood, surrounded by gnarled trees. I was sweating from the heat and reeling with nervousness.

I entered Nafha's dimly lit room. Although it was packed with people, she shone like a star in the darkness, her eyes as bewitching as glistening jewels. Smoke flowed from an incense burner set into one of the walls and revived memories of the incense burner the priest swung hypnotically back and forth at Sunday mass in my own Catholic church at home. I sat on a battered piece of grey-green lino that barely covered the floor's cold, lifeless stone. Above me lay the exposed ceiling, an intricate maze of tree trunks weaved together, each of them only two inches in diameter. Tied together, they twisted and tugged at each other like a sea of slithering brown snakes. A fluorescent light hung precariously from a single wire, dangling in the centre of the room. Flies buzzed incessantly around it, struggling in the stifling, humid air.

Behind a cheap white laminate table sat Nafha. Her face was unveiled. She wore a black headband on top of a white scarf and a black piece of cloth that covered her jaw and ended just below her ruby red lips. She was young, around 27-years-old. She had a chiselled, smooth face, subtle soft skin and displayed an air of grace and inner calmness as she sat quietly on a black plastic chair. In an odd way she resembled a religious nurse, with her sparkling snow white veil and her sweet smile that revealed brilliant white teeth. Then she became witch-like, radiating her spiritual healing powers. The top half of her dress was black, the bottom a brilliant vermilion with intricate gold embossed floral designs sprayed around the outside. I was attracted, yet repelled, by her aura that filled the tiny room.

Her patients either sat cross-legged on the floor, or on what makeshift seats were available. Nearby, three black figures hovered on an old car seat, waiting patiently for their consultation. Nafha's right hand lay on the head of the veiled woman nearest to her. Closing her eyes, she softly whispered verses from the Koran, stopped, then unveiled the patient and shook her head from right to left. The sounds of her neck cracking reverberated around the room. It brought a terrified "Ugh" from those gathered around. Nafha wrote special messages on a cheap, school notepad and handed them to her patient. This was the magic these people had come from miles around to experience. The woman paid for her medicine, made a donation and thanked her for her kindness before leaving for her village.

Finally, it was my turn. Nafha told me that she knew in advance that I was coming. The spirits had told her that morning. With Ezzy translating, she explained that her full name was Nafha Hamad Abdul. She had lived in the region her whole life. Her family knew she was different from an early age because she was psychologically sick as a child. When she miraculously recovered at the age of 13, she felt as if she could see into the future. She began dreaming and would regularly go to hear the Koran being read in the mosque. Her family knew that her body was with them but that her mind was not. By the age of 14 her extraordinary talents were noticed by her closest friends and, as word spread, she began her healing practice.

She said she consulted the spirits in her mind and they gave her the answer to people's problems. The look in people's eyes testified to their devout belief in her. Nafha's reputation went much further than these mountains. On some days, Nafha's patients came from surrounding Muslim countries to meet this mystic wonder. Her powers as a healer would no doubt spread like wild fire after word got out that a westerner from the other side of the world had come to seek her help.

I had to tell Nafha my problems. I dared not look into the dark, bottomless black eyes which could mysteriously penetrate the human soul. I explained who my parents were. As I had none of their personal belongings to give her I wrote down their names, She concentrated for a while and spoke with the spirits who told her I had been carrying this pain since childhood. A bad spirit had frightened me and there was only one way to get rid of it. First, she handed me a tightly folded piece of paper wrapped in green plastic to give to my mother. She told me that my mother should carry this close to her at all times. Nafha then handed me a cigarette with hand written magic lettering all over it, saying it must be smoked immediately.

Her next diagnosis was not a spoonful of sugar, but a red hot poker. Nafha's assistant stoked the fiery hot coals in a silver coated mini-furnace, the details of the mosque at Yifrus clearly embossed on its outside. Trance like, she walked towards me and as her doll-like hands sensually came up to me, her scarlet nail-polish glistened amongst fingers decked with gold rings and arms with jangling bracelets. She placed her left hand on the side of my head for support. With the thumb and third finger of her right hand she gently traced a line from my nose where the red hot poker would burn the middle of my head. Whispering *Qur'anic* verses into my ear, my flesh started to sizzle as the steel pierced my skin. The pain was so extreme I blacked out.

Nafha forced the second of the healing markings into the middle of my stomach and the smell of burning flesh aroused me. I exhaled a huge breath and opened my eyes. I was still in that dark, cavern-like room, but I felt like I was floating in a dream. The warmth from the hot steel enveloped me and I felt calm. Voices faded into a void. Nafha raised her right hand to her mouth, kissed her second finger and gently stroked my wounds, to seal them with her magic.

She returned to her table and scribbled the secret spiritual letters onto pieces of paper which were to cure me. She raised her head only briefly, then a brusque demand sent her young attendant scurrying to a small wooden cupboard for a heavy bag of traditional natural medicines to drink and potions to rub onto my body. Nafha nodded twice and bade me farewell. Her final words to me were: "I can help you, but you must help me too".

Ominous, thick, grey clouds were rolling over the valley as I stared out of the car window at Nafha's fast disappearing home. The wet season was coming and would bring new life to the barren land of Yemen. As nightfall descended, and the car bounced down jagged roads, I fell asleep from sheer exhaustion. In my head the country flashed before me — hand-carved terraces on mountains slopes; veiled women whose colourful robes blew in the breeze as they escorted their children and their goats home; men praying; young boys playing soccer in a dusty dry field and tiny kerosene lamps dotting the valley.

Somewhere between Nafha's house and Taiz, that 30 foot black snake came back into my dreams. But now Nafha had come to me, and this time the snake turned away and vanished into the abyss. In Taiz I raced into the hotel and ran a hot salty bath, both as part of my medicine, to remove the sticky oil from my body and soothe the three sets of scars which covered around four inches of my body.

I reached into the bar fridge and removed an ice cold bottle of water. Into it I slipped the first of Nafha's secret hand written messages. The folded, bundle of paper sank slowly into the water. Bit by bit, ink began streaming from Nafha's magic words, turning the sterilised water into a soft shade of blue. As I lifted the bottle to my lips I wondered if the Western world was truly myth-informed. Already I felt I could feel her healing powers seeping into my veins.

A Tale of Two Irans

by Peter Carty

My Iranian experience was in two parts: one in Iran, the other in London. The division was undesirable but unavoidable, essential even if I was to gain an insight into Iran, its people and its politics. Visiting Iran would educate me about the country and some, at least, of the people. But it was also necessary for me to travel elsewhere. Machinations by the British and Iranian establishments made it extremely difficult, if not impossible, to interview victims and opponents of the regime in Iran itself and without talking to them, I would not learn the reality of Iranian politics which confronted many Iranians.

The duality of this story and its displacements reflect the nature of Iran, a country that is, variously, a *diaspora* and a repressive state as well as a vast and diverse geographical area containing some of the world's most interesting and exciting cultures.

My journey began somewhat improbably, with a trip on London Underground's northern line to North Finchley, one of the capital's more nondescript inner suburbs. Its main street is a major traffic route, bordered by expanses of grey pavement and retail frontages.

One such outlet was Furnitureland, part of a London chain which, rather confusingly, sells carpets — none of them Persian. Above Furnitureland was another land — IranAid, a charity set up to assist victims of the Iranian regime. Unfortunately, the organisation was moribund, crippled by British charity regulators who stopped its operations and handed over its administration to a receiver, claiming it had funded terrorism in Iran. IranAid's supporters said the regulators were sent in by a UK Government keen to curry favour with the Iranian regime in order to foster lucrative trade deals. The staff and supporters were busy mounting a sit-in, to ensure that its records of operatives and recipients in Iran did not fall into the wrong hands.

The premises retained their original 1970's office fittings — swathes of formica and chocolate brown commercial carpet. Tea and cake were set out and 38-year-old Fatima told me her story. Her face was like a ripe pear, adorned with a fleshy nose. She wore a blue-patterned scarf wrapped round her head and neck, and a long-sleeved mustard shirt. Despite her opposition to the regime, her allegiance to her culture and religion remained. When I proffered my hand she declined it and apologised, explaining that handshakes were not her custom.

Fatima had fled Tehran with her two children 10 months earlier after prolonged harassment. "My husband assisted the families of other victims of the regime and publicised his dissatisfaction with its record on human rights," she said. "He was hounded and eventually vanished into prison. Before his detention I remember him being badly beaten in a park by the religious police for wearing a short-sleeved shirt."

Her water supply was regularly cut off. When she complained the bullying intensified. The day after her husband was taken to prison they attacked her and one of her sons. "They beat me with their hands and feet, kicked me and pulled my hair." She did not know what had happened to her husband since his imprisonment. "I suspect he has been killed, but we don't know."

It was too dangerous to try and openly leave Iran, so Fatima and her children were smuggled across the Turkish border. "One of my friends, Ghamar, was arrested at Tehran airport two weeks ago," she said. "She was charged with trying to leave the country. She was not political, all she wanted was a comfortable and honourable life. You can imagine the destiny of those who are in real opposition to the regime."

The economy was under strain and poverty was rampant. "Even many families who were middle class are living under severe pressure. They don't have enough food and are living miserable lives. I cannot go back to Iran," said Fatima. "I have told officials here 'kill me rather than send me back'."

Fatima's story and the tales of some of her fellow refugees gave me serious doubts about travelling to Iran, but I was swayed by a new President who gained a large majority in semi-democratic elections. The country's history was a roll call of empire after empire, dynasty after dynasty bloodily rising and collapsing — Elamites, Aryans, Achaemenians, Alexander the Great, Seleucids, Parthians, Sassanians, Arabs, Turks, Mongols, Timurids, Safavids, Afghans, Ghajars and Pahlavis — with the Persians all the while struggling to get on with their lives. With some misgivings, I headed to Heathrow.

I would like to tell you how I went to Iran and tracked down Fatima's relatives and the families of other victims I spoke to in Finchley. But the Charity Commission had made this — a quest which would be difficult at the best of times — impossible. All records of IranAid's beneficiaries were firmly locked away and its staff were taking no chances.

The first sign that I was entering a different culture came when a stewardess announced that no-one should bring alcohol into Iran, or 'doubtful magazines'. I could live without magazines, but travelling in a country without easy access to alcohol would be a challenge. I realised that one of Iran's roles would be to act as an enormous health farm.

As we landed the female passengers swathed their heads in scarves and donned *chadors* or overcoats. We were entering the world's only *shi-ite* muslim state. A state where women must remain covered so men are not lured into fornication, and where punishments for adultery, alcohol consumption and other transgressions are laid down in holy writ are painstakingly and painfully carried out.

Stepping off the plane, my nose tried to tell me that I was still in Finchley. I was immediately aware of heavy pollution. The smells were at odds with the surroundings. Tehran lies below the snow-capped Alborz mountains and the metropolis has a picture postcard backdrop. But the mountains have acted as a barrier, trapping the pollution from the regiments of Paykans (the omnipresent local vehicle modelled on the Hillman Hunter). The rush hour began at 7am, and from my hotel balcony the cars endlessly re-configured into fresh patterns, bacteria multiplying in a massive urban petri-dish.

My first stop was the White Palace, one of the Shah's old residences and now known as the People's Palace. It was surprisingly modest in size, though the same could not be said of the fittings. Despite the money lavished on the palace, kitsch was predominant — rich Persian carpets could not disguise their swirliness; mahogany panelling resembled veneer; overstuffed settees sang in choruses in beige; and every expensive ornament had an obvious desire to transform itself into a lava lamp.

The Shah was ousted after a mass revolt against his corruption and repression, though his dwelling made me suspect that his real crimes were against soft furnishings. The revolution and the Shah's approach to interior decor were not wholly unrelated, his tastes implying a scant regard for his subjects and their culture. A carelessness, which in a more important context, led to an unusually stressful house removal.

No trace of his dynasty lingered at street level. Posters of Khomeini and Rafsanjani were displayed in most shops and stalls, and on massive posters embellished with Farsi slogans: "Every martyr is an emblem of the honour of the revolution". The Iran-Iraq war ended in 1988, but remains fresh in the memories of Iranians. Every so often I was confronted with calm gazes from the gigantic visages of young men reproduced in enormous murals and revered as martyrs. A common image was that of a 13-year-old boy who tied dynamite to himself and hurled himself under a tank.

The largest cultural clash came from the sight of women. In scarves and chadors, they were everywhere. They were in the rear of buses in black, in contrast to the more colourfully garbed men in the front — an eerie reprise of racially segregated public transport in southern US states in the early 1960s. As part of a general loosening of society, the dress code for women was beginning to relax. Embroidered *roupushes* and colourful head scarves were appearing, although a western woman accompanying me was asked to re-secure her scarf when she went bareheaded in the streets.

The *chadors* effects were not uniform. There were circumstances where it conferred a kind of invisibility. Women walked around in large numbers, by themselves and in groups, until late into the evening. Partly, perhaps, as a result of the dress code, the streets seemed to be safer for them after dusk than thoroughfares in Western countries.

The evening bustle was surprising given the austere images of Iranian culture in the Western media. In the absence of bars and nightclubs, entertainment took place in restaurants. Live music was banned in the immediate wake of the revolution, but in recent years the regime's ongoing liberalisation meant traditional music was tolerated. In an eating house in a Tehran park I listened to Dervish music, sung by an old man clad in a white cassock, an embroidered waistcoat and a black skull cap. The drummer rang a tiny bell hanging from the ceiling to measure the singer's wailing sufi chants.

The clear tone of the drummer's bell contrasted sharply with the screeching klaxon of the alarm I heard later that day in the crown jewels vault in the centre of town. Iran has a surfeit of gems on public display in the vault, many acquired by the Shah. The sight of endless and excessive Liberace-style ornamentation only reinforced my impression of the last regime's taste deficiency. The alarm sounded and the front gates automatically swung shut whenever any of the display cases are touched. The klaxon sounded constantly, at least once every five minutes. It was going off so often I could not resist setting it off myself, and then, for the benefit of a nearby security guard, staring accusingly at a group of school children. Part of the collection consisted of jewel encrusted *hookahs*. My guide was keen to play down any suggestions of their misuse with suitably pious zeal.

"What were they used for smoking?" I asked him.

"Tobacco and other things."

"What, hashish?"

"No, no, no ... just tobacco."

There were long metal pipes encrusted with gold and jewels.

"Are those opium pipes?"

"No, no, no."

Cafes are as popular as restaurants on the social scene. In Tehran intellectuals and young people frequent Cafe Naderi. It was here that I was approached by Taher Rahmani, a 29-year-old graphic designer.

"I studied in Sheffield," he said. "But I like it here; life is good. I enjoy listening to live traditional music but I don't have any trouble getting hold of tapes of western music — Pink Floyd is my favourite."

He was smartly dressed and said that restrictions on fashion and other cultural areas had become more relaxed since the end of the Iran-Iraq war. Nevertheless, life in Iran was not all good.

"There is massive unemployment here," he said, "it is very difficult, even for university graduates to get work." A sluggish economy, independent traders who keep their capital abroad and enormous population increases have caused widespread joblessness.

The Iranians I met were extremely friendly and hospitable, partly because these qualities are firmly embedded in their culture and partly because they had encountered few foreigners for the last two decades. It became possible to gain individual tourist visas to Iran about 18 months before my visit, and while groups had been allowed in for longer, their interactions with locals were fewer and less spontaneous.

I was booked on an internal flight from Tehran to Shiraz, but when I arrived at the airport my plane had already left. The departure time had been brought forward by an hour — a common practice I was told. As I resigned myself to a night on a plastic chair in the departure lounge or on the floor if I was lucky enough to find a quiet spot, I was surprised by an invitation to rest in the prayer room. Relaxing on the comfortable carpets, watched over by a caretaker who got little sleep himself, busy as he was letting people in and out, my preconceptions of a fundamentalist abhorrence of outsiders softened further.

Other notions, this time of the homogeneous nature of the Iranian people, began to dissipate the next day on the highway from Shiraz to the ancient historic site of Persepolis. Next to this modern transport link, along which stormed brightly decorated lorries, a group of Khamse tribes people had pitched their tents.

Their leader was called Kian (King). "We've been trekking for 20 days," he said, "from a town near the Persian Gulf. It will take us another 10 days to reach the village where we want to spend a few months."

The Khamse are Turkish-speaking and possess beautiful but un-Iranian sounding names. One of Kian's companions was Mah Zarif ('Delicate Moon'). She was 32, but the rigours of nomadic life had aged so that she looked around 50. Others were Gol Afshan ('A Person Who Spreads Flowers') and Jan Afrouz ('A Flame of Life'). The older Khamse lived in tents made from woven goats hair blankets which were dyed black. Their younger companions favoured army surplus canvas dwellings. But some aspects of tradition showed no signs of succumbing to external influences — all of the women's colourful clothes were part of their marriage dowries.

The Khamse were shepherding a few goats and several hundred sheep, from which the women sheared wool for weaving into rugs that the men took into towns and sold. Their awareness of the value of money seemed limited, and they frequently let the rugs go for coppers. Their lifestyle was picturesque but hard. The Iranian Government has jurisdiction over more than eight major nomadic groups and is trying to place them in villages where they are more easily controllable.

The Khamse stood out from the general population, but then so did I.

Being a foreign novelty had its drawbacks in the towns and cities. Teenage girls in particular, laughed and giggled uncontrollably at the sight of a long-haired, green-eyed alien. In the courtyard of Shiraz's Friday Mosque a group of chador-clad schoolgirls asked if they could take a photograph of me. A young Iranian immediately approached. "Can my friend take a picture of me standing with you?" he asked. "I like having my picture taken with foreigners." It was a reversal of the normal 'tourist-snaps-interesting-looking-local' scenario and recurred frequently.

Strolling through Shiraz's bazaar I discovered that unlike every other underdeveloped country I had visited, counterfeit jeans did not form a bulwark of the market stall economy. Instead, locals invented brand names including, with novel incongruity, 'Sanyo Jeans' and 'Boscht Jeans'. Further into the bazaar a pet shop sold baby chicks dyed in lurid hues of pink, green, purple and orange. The chicks rarely survived long with their new owners, especially in the summer when they expired in the heat after a couple of weeks. Music stalls sold cassettes openly, something which would have seemed outlandish even 18 months ago, and in the butcher's section calves heads were neatly laid out in mini Damien Hirst-style displays. Most bizarre of all, no-one tried to sell me anything; the stall holders were not yet accustomed to viewing tourists as fresh meat.

Trolleys rushed up and down the bazaar alleyways, together with bicycles and motor scooters, rendering passage hazardous. Traversing the streets outside was much more life threatening. Pedestrians loped along the pavements, eyed by lolling shopkeepers, but the real activity took place out on the tarmac. Crossing roads involved jumping out and hoping the vehicles would slow sufficiently for me to thread between them. The traffic rhythms were different to London, and I had to shadow other pedestrians, keeping them between myself and the oncoming traffic.

This meant loitering around for people to come along and step from the kerb. On one occasion I waited hopefully behind two seven or eight-year-old girls and ventured out after them. After a few steps they climbed into a cab, leaving me distraught and at the mercy of the cars. Another day, I saw a traffic policemen bobbing in the metallic surf. He was feinting from side to side, occasionally holding up a hand for appearances' sake.

Esfahan is perhaps Iran's most beautiful city. Its star building is the Masjed-é Emam mosque — an Islamic echo of St. Pauls with vaults, arches and domes. But I found some of the bridges over the Zayande river more striking. There are five, and the best designed have the appearance of truncated aqueducts, some with tea-houses built into their arches. The words 'classic' and 'timeless' are greatly over-used by writers, but the spare lines and clean, sand brickwork of the 17th century Khaju and Chubi bridges could be the designs of leading contemporary architects back in London.

The teahouse on Chubi bridge has alcoves where I sat drinking tea, sucking on a hookah and watching the river rushing around me. There were Persian carpets on the floor and walls, coloured globes hung from the ceiling and a small scale model of a mosque complete with illuminated lights was a fixture. The decor was not as diverting, however, as that of another local tea-house which sports pictures of Adolf Hitler on its walls — the owner admires strong leaders.

A man sidled up. He was an engineer, and invited me to a party. His spoken English was not fluent, so he wrote sentences on a piece of paper: "Muslims. X. (I think the cross signified disapproval). I am not a muslim. Come to party." I didn't go because I was otherwise engaged, but my presence in the tea house attracted attention from other patrons. I completed a mini-disc recording, and was accosted as I left by another man, who had also studied in Sheffield like Taher Rahmani in Tehran.

He wore a smart suit and was accompanied by an attractive Iranian woman. "I saw you taping some material in the tea-house and I approve of your work as a journalist," he said. "But there are conservative people who would not."

It was an evening of chance encounters. As I tried to hail a taxi in the darkness, a man whose coiffure carried a hint of mullet offered me drugs. "Hashish, opium, heroin. Come and try my *hookah*."

He had remarkable eyesight. "Your eyes are red, have you already been smoking?"

I resorted to mime to attempt to explain that my roseate corneas were the result of contact lens irritation, rather than substance abuse.

Back in the Masjed-é Emam mosque, I turned a corner and encountered around 20 schoolgirls, all 15 to 16-years-old and immaculately dressed in blue veils and black *chadors*, a flock of starlings swooping together and parting as they sang out questions and answers.

When asked what they wanted to do in adult life they said,

"I want to be a lawyer."

"A doctor."

"An engineer."

"Don't you want to get married?" I asked.

"No, nooooh, noooooooh."

"What kind of music do you like?"

"The Spice Girls!"

"The Backstreet Boys!"

"And do you like football?"

"Yes! Yes! Yes!"

"Your favourite team?" I asked.

There was a lull as they gathered breath.

"MANCHESTER UNITED," they cried in unison.

The next evening I visited a place favoured by young people, the Nikan cafe and restaurant. One year ago the existence of an American-style diner with piped music would have been unthinkable, yet here it was — complete with pictures of Khomenei and Rafsanjani gazing sternly down at the customers. For less than £2 I enjoyed a steak *chateaubriand*, chips and salad. The *maitre d'* came by a couple of times to check that everything was to my liking, followed by the head chef who stressed that he had been trained in France. He was at pains to offer me a drink on the house, though rather than a large brandy I received a cup of tea.

In the pilgrimage centre of Mashhad, the luxurious Homa Hotel displayed a large 'Down With USA' slogan above its entrance. I saw a similar sign outside the former premises of the US embassy in Tehran. The placards were relics of a more strife-laden era of US-Iran relations. Even during the revolution and its immediate aftermath, Khomeini emphasised that Iran's hostility was directed toward the US Government, not the people. Links were being steadily restored and US tour groups now visited. A tiny, wizened old Canadian tourist with spiky white hair and wearing a Hawaiian shirt stared at the Homa Hotel's sign. "These people sure have the right idea about Americans," he said.

Iran sprang a final surprise when I travelled up to the Turkmenistan steppes in north-east Iran, with the aim of visiting the ancient remains at Khaled Nabi. It was a lengthy journey, with a final section over dirt roads that passed through fields of wheat, barley and cumin laid out over a flat plain. The landscape generated strange resonances of East Anglia — though a camel tethered outside a house rapidly dispelled that illusion.

Vast gorges opened up on one side of the road before the main act began. The steppes reared up, enormous sand dunes rolling towards the plain of central Asia, everywhere and nowhere to the nomadic groups who have coursed back and forth across it for thousands of years. A short drive into the dunes brought me to the Khaled Nabi site where the steppes can be seen, a giant frozen sea stretching away in all directions.

The site takes its name from the individual who discovered it in the 4AD. Accounts of him vary: some say he was a Nestorian Christian, others that his allegiances were Islamically inclined, despite pre-dating Mohammed by four centuries. To reach the site I negotiated narrow paths that sometimes skirted long drops. I needed two guides on either side holding my hands to guide me over the most difficult stretches. I'm glad I persevered. I was astonished to encounter a field full of prehistoric stone penises. There were dozens of phalluses, between four and six feet tall and sculpted from a basalt-like rock.

Many of the penises are in their original positions, pointing to the sky. What they symbolise can only be speculated upon. The rock from which they have been hewn does not originate locally, so it can be safely guessed that creating and transporting then involved massive exertion. Little research has been done into their history and scientific studies were abandoned after the revolution.

My journey of discovery ended here, on the Central Asian steppes in the middle of a field of penises, a long way away from Finchley geographically, and as far removed from it culturally as is possible.

Most of my ideas about Iran had changed by the time I left. Sometimes Iranians would ask, "What do people in England think of Iran?" or "What do people in Britain say about the Iranian people?" and I would dissimulate embarrassedly. I could not tell them the popular perspective was one of fundamentalism and religious, bloodthirsty fanatics. The Iranian Government seemed to be becoming ever more relaxed, and in many parts of the country sightings of the formerly feared religious police, the Komité, were rare.

I cannot leave you with a single picture of Iran. I travelled on a journey that was not continuous and did not return to its point of departure. I am, though, left with an overriding impression of the Iranians that owes less to modern mathematics and more to my immersion in their history and monuments, and in particular their shrines. I spent hours in the country's most inspiring mosques, all of them containing planes and curves composed of millions of tiles, each one individually a fragment, fractured and scattered, and yet in concert diffusing an unforgettable harmony.

Cursed in the City of the Dead

by Juliet Coombe

The dunes rippled in the golden afternoon sunlight. Like giant rattlesnakes they swirled and vanished over the horizon, hissing as the northerly breeze whipped up the sand around my ankles. Mohammed, my camel, was definitely no saint. Snorting, he tugged at his reins, irritated by the slow, repetitive pace of those in front who kept stopping to take photographs.

Horse breeders had their Arabian steeds out for a spot of late afternoon training as our camel chain rode past the ancient Egyptian Pyramids of Giza, one of the 'Seven Wonders of the World'. You would think a sunset jaunt into the desert would be a romantic fantasy come true. Thoughts of a passionate rendezvous under a swaying palm tree, however, could not have been further from my mind. My thoughts were still with thousands of women forced, due to poverty, to live in Cairo's twelve ancient cemeteries.

Their homes in the southern and northern graveyards are bleak and forbidding, particularly at night when grave-robbers and drug-runners abound. Lying at the foot of the dusty Muqattam hills, the jumble of buildings, each one a family burial plot, resemble semi-detached houses. This was not a cemetery as I understood it. The tombs held a mysterious, even haunting appeal. Their fascination lies in the decaying beauty of burial chambers that date back to the 12th Century and the famous bodies that lie beneath their cenotaphs.

Tombs like that of the Armenian slave Shaggar al-Durr. Her plastered brick and stucco mausoleum commands as much respect as its deceased owner once did. A woman of beauty and cunning, Shaggar called herself Queen of all Egypt when her husband died, in order to protect the throne for her son who was fighting in Iraq. Often compared to Cleopatra, she ruled for 80 days. The first and last female Islamic ruler in Egypt. She was violently murdered with wooden bath clogs in 1257 when her deception was uncovered. After being killed, her body thrown to the dogs and jackals in the ancient citadel. For many of the women who live in the graveyards she is considered a heroine, a person whose burial chamber with its simple mother of pearl mosaic sums up death perfectly in one simple, prophetic verse: "O ye who stand beside my grave, show not surprise at my condition, yesterday I was as you. Tomorrow you will be as me."

Shaggar's words sent a shiver down my spine as my camel and I rode through the ever changing dunes. As the sand shifted in the wind, it changed the patterns of the well worn Bedouin tracks, making them disappear altogether in places. My impatient camel quickened its pace, and I found myself absorbed, not by the majestic surroundings of the ancient Pharaohs' Pyramids, but the purported inscription on Tutankhamun's tomb: "Death shall come on swift wings to him that toucheth the tomb of Pharaoh."

Surely the mysterious deaths of Lord Carnarvon and his crew of archaeologists should have been a lesson about the dangers of entering the tombs and tangling with the spirit underworld. Marie Corelli, an English authority on such matters, warned only weeks before Carnarvon entered the burial chamber of Tutankhamun in early February 1922 that: "The most dire punishment follows any rash intruder into a sealed tomb". On the official opening day of the tomb, on 28 February 1922, the chief archaeologist Howard Carter's pet canary was swallowed by a giant cobra, similar to the one on the Pharaoh's brow that spits fire and poison at his enemies.

Carter dismissed the curses, saying: "All sane people should dismiss such inventions with contempt", but he could never fully explain the catalogue of bizarre deaths that occurred to his men after the opening of the boy King's burial chamber. On entering the inner sanctum he said: "I could see nothing, the hot air escaping from the chamber caused the candle flame to flicker, but as my eyes grew accustomed to the light, details of the room within emerged slowly, from the mist strange animals, statues and gold — everywhere the glint of gold." Seconds later the candle blew out and Lord Carnarvon, who accompanied him panicked, coughing and spluttering from the lack of air as he stumbled back to the surface.

Around this time Carnarvon was bitten by a mosquito and the bite became badly infected when he cut himself shaving. Suffering from high fevers he dreamt of being ripped apart by an eagle's talons. On April 5 he died and the lights of Cairo are said to have inexplicably gone out, whilst in England his dog Susie simultaneously joined her master in the afterlife, further fuelling the power of the alleged curse. World headlines read: "The curse of the mummy strikes again", igniting international terror and a revival of superstitious beliefs in Egypt.

It was these weird events in the Valley of the Kings that left most Egyptians in no doubt that one should not desecrate the tombs of the dead, only admire them from afar. My Egyptian translator was so superstitious that she refused to enter any of the Sultans' or Amirs' mausoleums in Cairo's Northern cemetery. "It is dangerous to do so," she said, her eyes so full of fear. I didn't ask her to elaborate. She tried to persuade me to change my plans and go and see the Egyptian museum in the centre of town, but I was determined to find out more about this little known enclave that I discovered by accident on a previous visit.

It was on that last visit to Cairo that a friend suggested going to Al Khalifa, Cairo's live animal market. The market was smelly and noisy, but I was enthralled by the goings on, particularly watching the donkey cart owners loading herds of sheep into their tiny trailers. Sitting around sipping sweet mint tea I learnt about the complex art of buying and selling goats, cows, sheep and pigeons, a bartering process that can take several hours. Wandering off I accidentally stumbled on to a mysteriously silent and spooky-looking street. I found myself in an area radically different from the rest of Cairo.

The houses were geometrically patterned and had large domes. Most of the doors were double padlocked and the inner courtyards empty and dark. I pushed my face against a set of railings to get a clearer view inside and was startled by a creaking door. A mischievous girl in pigtails, holding a crumbling skull in her doll-like hands appeared out of the darkness. At first I thought she was playing a game of hide and seek, but her tiny bare feet and torn dress suggested otherwise. This was the 'City of the Dead' and the little girl's home. Skeletons and rubbish had become her toys. Inside other tombs I found children playing with toy trucks made from plastic water bottles with Coca Cola cans attached so they could wheel them around. They seemed oblivious to the fact that they were using their ancestors tombs as a playground.

In Cairo, burdened by overcrowding, there is no real public housing and the number of people moving into the cemeteries is increasing. In ten years the figure has grown from a few hundred to more than 50,000. As early as the 15th Century people inhabited Cairo's cemeteries, originally as paid guards, employed to maintain family plots and prepare them for burials, birthdays and Muslim feasts. Not wanting to live alone, many brought their families from the villages to join them, swelling these small communities generation after generation.

The Minister of Tourism now wants to move these people on. He is embarrassed by their presence and under pressure from rich Egyptians who constantly push for their eviction. The tragic reality is that single and divorced women continue to occupy the ancient memorials because no other options are provided. The homeless Egyptian women are angry about being forced to live in this bleak and terrifying place. "The rich only think of the condition of their ancestors graves and forget that the Prophet saw mothers and children as a major priority," one explained. "The government in Cairo should find a way to help us and our families instead of constantly condemning the way we live, which is no choice of our own."

The memory of the womens' plight remained etched in my memory from this first trip and I was determined to find out more about the people who live there and are seen by Cairo's elite as social outcasts and witches who collaborate with international skeleton thieves in the illicit trade of selling exhumed bodies.

My translator on this second visit found the place shocking, distressing and unclean, refusing to drink even a cup of coffee offered to her by one of the families we talked to. Their generosity left me humbled and saddened, considering the small amount they had to live on. Many seemed strangely resigned to their fate. "We are like an extended family, if one of us gets sick we all chip in so she can go to hospital," said Fatima, pointing to one of the graves that had been turned into a medical drop-in centre. The area was like a self-contained village with a daily market in Qayt-bey, a police station and a post office.

The translator repeatedly told me no-one lived in the graveyards, but beside them in high rise flats. At one stage she refused to get out of the car, saying it was, "dangerous and disrespectful to the dead to continue with my line of questioning". Questions to find out how many people lived in the cemeteries and whether they feared angering their ancestors' spirits by turning the tombs into their homes.

Maybe I should have listened to her, particularly after one group of Egyptian women at Qayt-bey — the last great Mamuluk leaders' mausoleum, and one of the most interesting parts of the City of the Dead — threw their hands in the air and cursed me. Wearing black *milayas* (dresses) and thick, laced head scarves, the women were huddled around a red hot brazier like the three witches from Macbeth. Shrouded in thick woollen blankets despite the high temperature, their weather beaten faces and knotted grey hair should have been warning enough. They cursed me several more times in Arabic as I emerged from exploring the inner vestibule of his tomb. They accused me of not revering their ancestors, despite the fact that they had made these memorials their homes, turning the tomb stones into dining room tables and hanging pink frilly underwear on washing lines between the head stones.

On one cenotaph, bowls of rice and vegetables were being served to a couple of hungry teenagers. Richard Parker in his book 'Islamic Monuments in Cairo' says we should look at this custom through Egyptian eyes, not Western ones: "The practice of picnicking with the dead has been remarked on by many foreign visitors. It is not difficult to see a connection with the ancient Egyptian pre-occupation with the after-life. There is no distinction between leaving food in a tomb to be consumed after death and preparing and eating food next to the tomb as a gesture to the dead."

The women's angry taunts and the wagging of one dirty finger continued to haunt me on my two-hour camel ride through the desert. Slowly our caravan disappeared behind a series of rolling sand dunes. Just as the sun was about to set, Mohammed, excessively bored by the slow, meandering pace of the other camels, decided to tear away from the group, bucking in every direction to rid himself of me. Tossing my body in the air, I somersaulted twice, spinning like a coin. Would it be heads or tails? Colours spun before my eyes and then everything went silvery grey. I bounced off a rock and into the sand, then blacked out.

I woke face down on a cold white slab. To all intents and purposes my surroundings looked like the inside of an Egyptian tomb with its smooth empty white washed walls. My body was in agonising pain. I tried to move, but nothing happened. All I could see between flashing lights were the old women from the graveyard cackling at me.

As the x-ray was switched off, I realised that I was in As-Salam International Hospital. My jumbled thoughts began to clear and I could make out intent Arabic voices. Men in white coats appeared from behind a screen and a torch was shone in my eyes. Taking my hand, they pulled my fingers in every direction. I screamed in pain as they cracked the bone back into its socket.

With a silver cast on my finger I was discharged several hours later. My back was also bruised, but at least I was fully intact. Hobbling slowly out of the hospital, I was met by an unusual welcoming committee — a chorus of bleating sheep. Cairo's balconies had been transformed into makeshift farmyard pens in preparation for the annual *Eid al-Adha* Muslim feast.

After several pain killers, I finally fell asleep. I woke the next day to a city full of hundreds of thousands of sheep, cows, goats and a few camels. I became quite fond of the inner city farmyard sounds, they made a refreshing change from the continual honking of car horns. At the weekend I woke at 6am to silence. Not a bleat could be heard anywhere. Every animal had been slaughtered as the sun rose over Cairo. One third of the meat was handed out to the poor, whilst the remaining two-thirds were cooked for a massive celebratory meal. The festival is a public holiday in Egypt, and the now empty business sector, where the sheep and goats had been slaughtered, was covered by large pools of blood. The festival had aroused my curiosity and I braved a return to the northern cemetery. The place was totally transformed by the days festivities.

The cemetery was packed with pilgrims paying their respect to the dead. There were cars with blood-stained hand prints splattered all over the vehicles to ward off the evil eye and protect the owners new property in the forthcoming months. Traffic around the area was at a standstill as different forms of transport carried thousands of mourners. People were still dipping their fingers into the freshly cut necks of slaughtered sheep and smearing hand prints, dripping with blood, across one bonnet after another. In many of the cars, the Qur'an sat in the front window like a shrine as the blood dripped onto the hard baked ground.

On day two of *Eid al-Adha* it seemed like all of Cairo, all 18 million inhabitants, had descended on the graveyard to pay their respects to the deceased. For many who cannot afford to make the journey to Mecca, this spiritual day is seen as a vital one in the Muslim calendar, acting as an alternative religious pilgrimage. The south winds howled and sand swirled around my head, as black veiled women came from all directions in packed donkey carts, lamenting the souls of their ancestors.

The usually padlocked mausoleums were now open. Inside I caught glimpses of numerous extended families wailing and throwing themselves onto the cold slabs of the tomb's stone. Moved by the sadness of death, and feeling as though I was intruding, I quickly wandered on, disappearing into the mass of street vendors selling everything from hot bread to cold drinks. Everywhere I looked flowers were being made into wreaths, whilst wicker baskets full of steaming bread were given away to the poor. Old men smoked *shisha* water pipes with a rich mix of tobacco and honey, exchanging family news between puffs. At the end of the street a mobile drinks stand sold Coca Cola, bringing a new meaning to the slogan 'Coke adds life'. Sheep and goats skins lay discarded in front of the wrought iron gates, left over from the 6am slaughter. On one corner a couple of small boys had wrapped themselves up in the skins and fallen asleep, oblivious to the hundreds of thousands of people who passed by.

The air was full of chatter and the chanting of the Qur'an could be heard inside the vestibules of the family mausoleums, a series of elaborate sections where the deceased bodies, often a complete family from several generations ago, were interred in a huge underground chamber. They are usually not covered with earth or mummified like the Pharaohs, just wrapped in crisp white muslin and laid out on the ground, their faces towards the holy city of Mecca. Above ground is a memorial to the deceased. In the wealthiest grave sites there are a series of outhouses and a stone staircase leading into the central burial area, which is concealed by a large stone or marble slab. These are only removed when another member of the family is buried.

Old men wearing dark blue galabayas sat watching TV, their aerials attached to grave stones. I stopped and talked to some of the permanent inhabitants. The more enterprising younger women explained that they took in washing, made carpets and sewed cotton sacks to eke out a living and cover the basic costs like bread and beans. Rashar, one woman who lives in the graveyard said: "Cairo's social set may see us as outcasts who are disrespectful to the dead, defiling their graves by living there and should be forcibly moved on, but why don't they use their money to resolve the problem instead of taking drugs and buying fast cars."

An American expat who has lived in Cairo for more than 12 years, confirmed this. "At the height of the Sadat years, drug deals were regularly done in the grave yards." She fondly remembered the long hashish-induced nights in the City of the Dead, and wild parties when all the rules were openly broken. In any other part of the world there would have been a public out-cry, but in Cairo the graveyards are seen as the perfect place to hide drugs. As the police, like many Egyptians, are deeply superstitious about the consequences of searching a grave, they often turned a blind eye to what was going on.

I waited at the cemetery for Hassim, an Egyptian friend who was coming to see his recently deceased mother. Plastic bags from discarded bread donations circled around me like autumn leaves and fell to the ground, only to be picked up again by another gust of wind. Finally he arrived empty handed. I asked him why he had not brought flowers with him like so many other people I had seen. He told me that such things were not part of the Muslim faith, but came from the Pharonic tradition. As we walked through a maze of graves in shades of green, grey and sandstone, I passed generations of Egyptian families eating chick peas and pitta bread. Some of the tombs were strewn with freshly cut flowers. An adjacent name plaque revealed the date of the deceased, another tradition, which Hassim claimed, "deeply religious Muslims strongly oppose."

A sandstorm filled the air with thick dust and turned the sky silvery grey. I was deeply relieved when the guardian of Hassim's family grave unlocked the door to his tomb, allowing us to take refuge from the storm. As the weather-beaten wooden doors blew shut behind us, Hassim explained that more than 80 people were buried in this tiny room, women on the right and men on the left.

Taking the family's copy of the Qur'an out of its battered plastic covering, he asked for silence as he read out loud. I was mesmerised by the words. They sounded like enchanted music and it soothed my troubled mind. After he finished, I asked him to translate what he had said, but he explained that English failed to capture the true meaning of the verse. Back on the streets the atmosphere had transformed from one of sadness to a street party, with loud pop music blasting from tape recorders. People were dancing and singing for joy, encouraging me to join in the festivities.

I was invited by a family to eat some freshly slaughtered sheep in a thick brown bubbling broth. I resisted the sheep eye balls, a great Egyptian delicacy, but tucked into the broth with thick crusts of bread. As the day became night, people lit flares and bitter-sweet Egyptian wine was served from clay pots.

In the darkness, the City of the Dead appeared hauntingly out of the sand storm and the spirits of the Amirs and Sultans gripped me. I felt apprehensive, but was determined to spend at least one night in the cemetery. To give myself courage, I drank another cup of greenish wine, that tasted more like turpentine than alcohol. I continued to dance and drink the night away. As all the street stalls closed down and everyone went to bed, I decided to walk to the top of the hill and watch the sun rise across Cairo's Northern Cemetery. The Mameluke Necropolis of minarets and domes sparkled in the golden beams of light, breathing eternal life into the majestic marble tombs of the Egyptian Amirs, Sultans and ordinary citizens. Except for a couple of barking mongrel dogs, nothing stirred in Cairo's City of the Dead, not even the living.

On the Road to Damascus

by Matt Rudd

The rattle of machine-gunfire was all around. A car exploded and a man dressed in fatigues fell wounded from a roof top. Others dived for cover as a helicopter gunner strafed the scene with bullets. I couldn't believe I'd come all the way to Lebanon to find the A-team wreaking havoc on my television set. I switched it off and walked to the balcony to watch the noisy bustle of West Beirut instead.

I'd been in town for two days and was already confused. On one level, Beirut is a city looking to the West with its trendy bars, smartly dressed students and a casino straight out of Las Vegas. On another, it's very, very Middle Eastern. Even today the word 'Beirut' is a synonym for war and the battle scars are still evident. When I asked a Dutch diplomat to explain the complexities of the place, he adapted what was originally a Russian observation; "Spend a day in Lebanon and you could write a book. Spend a week and you could only write a chapter. Spend a year and you won't be able to write a word." Nowhere else in the world do you have to step over an anti-tank barrier to get to a Hard Rock Café.

The paradoxes began at the airport. Three times as many Lebanese live overseas as at home and Beirut has a new, flashy terminal to reflect this international flavour. The scheme to upgrade the gateway to Beirut —

masterminded by billionaire and former prime minister, Rafiq Hariri — symbolises a determination to forget the horrors of the past. Still, I was escorted to the terminal by armed soldiers and when I stepped out the other side the first thing I saw was Haret Horaik, a *Shi-ite* area known as a recruiting ground for *Hezbollah*.

Then there is the challenge of getting from the airport to town. Outside the departure area I found myself in the taxi equivalent of the Grand Bazaar. I got rid of the first ten cabbies by claiming I was going with friends. As it became apparent that I had none however, the drivers became more persistent. They laughed when I mentioned buses and one particular enthusiastic driver gave me a well-rehearsed speech on government regulations when I mentioned 'service' or 'share taxis'. So despite my intentions of keeping to a shoestring budget, I found myself paying US$25 for a four kilometre ride in a 1974 Mercedes. Convincing the friendly con-artist to drive me to my hotel was an almost insurmountable challenge.

"So you have a hotel?" he asked.

"Yes thank you. Hotel Mushrek."

"Ahhh. This is not so good. Very expensive. Many dollars."

"Oh well."

"It's OK. I very happy to take you to beautiful and cheap hotel of my brother."

"No, that's very kind but I have a reservation at Mushrek. I'm fine."

"Good then. Special rate — it's not far."

And so it continued.

It is impossible to go to Beirut without any preconceptions, and if you go in search of the clichéd war image, it's easy to find. The infamous Green Line dividing the Christian East and Muslim West is easily identified by the bullet-riddled buildings and occasional shell craters. Walking along the line, you get a chilling image of two sides fighting each other from apartment blocks little more than 25 metres apart. On the subject of Holiday Inns, PJ O'Rourke somewhat irreverently asked, "Who has not fantasised about blowing one to flinders?" In Beirut, they did. The 1975 Battle of the Hotels was scene one of the first outbreaks of violence in the civil war. The Muslims were in the Holiday Inn, the Christians in the Hilton and that was the end of the Lebanese tourism industry.

Today, building sites have replaced bomb craters. Since 1992 the Government has been requisitioning properties in downtown Beirut that survived the war, levelling them and creating one of the world's largest reconstruction schemes. Despite having read about the Solidere project before I arrived, the sheer scale of it astonished me. The Place des Martyrs, once Beirut's central square, is a series of holes the size of office blocks and is destined to become the new central business district by 2006. Assuming, of course, that the money and peace continue.

Unfortunately peace is not guaranteed. For despite years of war, Lebanon's eighteen officially recognised religions are still allied to conflicting political and strategic ambitions. One Englishman who lived in Lebanon for several years described the new face of Beirut as a whitened sepulchre; a beautiful port city concealing a rotting core of sectarian hatred. Others consider that too pessimistic.

"I've spent my life worrying about things that never happened," said Bechara Namour.

Since the end of the war Lebanon's answer to Terence Conran has adopted a more optimistic approach, building a string of stylish hotels and restaurants in the exclusive francophile Achrafieh district of East Beirut. Now Namour is expanding along the coast to the Muslim West and is one of many entrepreneurs busily recreating the Riviera *chic* for which Beirut was once renowned.

I was surprised by this civilised twist to Beirut. The streets of mainly Christian Achrafieh are lined with chocolate shops, interior designers and fashion boutiques. The city is a gastronomic paradise, with the very best of European, traditional Lebanese and many types of Asian cuisine all within easy crawling distance of my hotel. Better still, coffee was never far away — surely a major factor when considering the merits of any city.

Beirut's admirable obsession with caffeine gave me many a happy hour sitting, Parisian-style, at pavement tables sipping espresso and indulging in the art of people-watching. My favourite was the Café de Paris. Somewhat at odds with other more fashionable establishments springing up across the city, it has remained practically unchanged since 1971. It's the kind of place where the staff have to sit at the tables to make it look busy. The piped medleys of 'Yesterday' and 'My Way' ensure customers don't stay long, but the coffee is excellent.

One afternoon I took a walk from the American University (AUB) to the Solidere building site along the Corniche. This sea-front walkway was battered by Lebanese, Syrian and Israeli bombardments and the resulting lack of palm trees bears witness to its tortured past. Now, however, it feels like Venice Beach as corpulent joggers plugged into Walkmans and cellular phones come out in the evenings. I was half-expecting Pamela Anderson to strut by in a red swimsuit until I saw a slaughtered sheep lying ceremonially in the doorway of a newly opened delicatessen. Two cultures collided as the wheels of rollerbladers drew lines on the pavement with the blood of the sacrificial lamb.

To prepare for my journey deeper into the Middle East I made a couple of forays into the Bekaa Valley, a high plain hemmed in by two sets of parallel mountains separating Beirut and Damascus. Although I haven't been to France for a while, I'm sure my wine tour was not the kind you'd expect in Bordeaux. On the way to Château Rothschild, for example, do the French army mount road blocks? Neither military checkpoints nor Hezbollah collection boxes obscure your view of any French vineyard, but then France is not at war with her southern neighbour.

"We had to smuggle corks over the mountains," said Michel de Bustros. "For two days in 1982 they were fighting over our land. It was a full-scale war, you know, with heavy artillery and fighter jets. Supply lines to Beirut were blocked and we had to do what we could."

The director of Lebanon's Château Kefraya was not the only vigneron to be affected, but being nearest to the Israeli border he was the first to see tanks tearing through his vines and ruining much of that year's crop. "It was heart breaking, but what can you do?" he said sadly. In the 1980s, several crops destined for Serge Hochar's world-renowned Château Musar were left to rot because pickers refused to risk sniper fire. When it was safe to pick the grapes they had to be checked for shrapnel.

On my second trip to Bekaa, I stopped at a Jesuit community just north of Chtaura to sample home-made yoghurt, cheese and bread. Until last year this peaceful institution had a Palestinian guerrilla training camp on part of its land, but an Israeli air attack shattered the peace — and many of the church windows.

"Were you badly hit?" I asked.

"Well, the buildings were okay, but the cows couldn't be milked for three days," said Fr. Briars. "That is a very long time." The old priest had lived through many of Lebanon's troubles over the last 30 years and knew how to grade each one. As we settled down to lunch on the edge of a dried up lake we could see Palestinians learning the intricacies of guerrilla fighting.

"They are okay," said the old priest. "And if I asked them to leave, how can we know who would replace them?"

After two weeks in Lebanon, more perplexed than ever but as acclimatised as I could hope to be, I continued my journey.

The road to Damascus was funded by the Syrian military and has the dubious honour of being the best road in Lebanon. Some suggest this might be connected to occasional urges by the Syrian Government to give its troops and tanks the chance to see the sea, and the new road means it is only three hours to Beirut. The two mountain ranges en route mean it is best travelled by day and in clear weather. So I wasn't in the calmest frame of mind when I arrived at Beirut's main taxi rank, at dusk and in a thunderstorm.

I had been warned that if I died in the Middle East it would be at the hands of a Syrian taxi driver rather than a frenzied terrorist. I didn't get the chance to choose my driver as I had hoped. Instead I was accosted by a forceful moustache who removed my passport, locked my pack in the boot of a bright yellow 1970s Dodge and promptly disappeared. After 30 minutes and still no sight of the moustache, I was convinced I had been fleeced and that my pack and passport were lost forever. But the moustache returned a while later with four other people wanting to go to Damascus. In the back sat an old man, a sickly child and a student-type who could speak English but wouldn't. In the front sat the driver and an obese man. I got the remaining inch-and-a-half .

As we veered through Beirut's rush-hour traffic, the horn clearly more important than the gears, I was breathing in time with my fellow passenger. Each time he inhaled, I exhaled and vice-versa. Leaving the safety of gridlock traffic behind, the pace increased and I repeatedly checked for a seat-belt that just wasn't there. Unaware of my growing concerns, my rotund neighbour tried to strike up a conversation. No matter how many times I politely demonstrated my lack of Arabic, he insisted on asking further questions.

We climbed recklessly into the Mount Lebanon range and above the snow-line. Since the only illumination on our vehicle was the right indicator, we had the element of surprise over oncoming traffic, only swerving when our driver could see the whites of their eyes. On one of the many hairpin bends I wasn't surprised to see a dazed driver surveying the wreckage of what had moments before been a BMW.

Perhaps this continual flirting with death is a psychological reaction to the civil war — the "if I can get through that I'll be fine driving like a maniac" philosophy. It would explain why boys do wheelies up and down the streets of Beirut on high-powered motorbikes. It would also explain why my driver was negotiating blind corners on an icy road at night, at the same speed I would drive in broad daylight on a dual carriageway.

We hurtled up past the turning to Aaley, a mainly Druse area where Walid Jumblat, the local warlord, played an intricate and often inflammatory part in the war, securing at one time or other the support of all the major participants.

"I used to collect tanks," said the former minister and present feudal overlord, with a smile, "but I stopped when the Russians gave me 50". Tanks from Russia, guns from the US and, according to former Israeli Prime Minister Shimon Peres, money from the Israelis. Now all he collects are cars and motorcycles, although many think his stocks of ammunition and weaponry explain his recent purchase of Château Kefraya.

"I am sure he finds the deep cellars very convenient," said one European diplomat.

Other peoples hobbies were the least of my worries as we chicaned down into the Bekaa. I never thought I'd be pleased to see a military checkpoint. But on this journey they provided brief moments of relative calm.

The Bekaa has two distinct types of checkpoint. The first are Lebanese, soldiers with multicoloured khaki uniforms and relaxed smiles. The second are Mukhabarat — Syrian secret police. They wear standard issue black leather jackets with Kalashnikov rifles draped casually across their shoulders, presumably so they will not stand out from the crowd. They tend not to smile. One diplomat I met said he slowed for the Lebanese but accelerated past the Syrians, determined to show his dislike for their presence. My driver showed more deference, but he didn't have the advantage of diplomatic plates.

We stopped at Chtaura, a small town which seemed to exist entirely as a shopping centre for Damascenes. People nip over the border for Western cigarettes, Coke, beer, TVs, washing machines and cars, or as a friend put it, "everything except sugar and salt". I felt as though I was in a neon update of the Wild West as I wandered from one bright shop to the next. This was not the kind of place you would spend any time getting to know, but my co-passengers relished the chance to stock up. After an hour, all remaining boot and leg-space duly packed with assorted goodies, we skidded away on the second leg of the white-knuckle ride, leaving a cloud of dust behind us.

The Lebanese-Syrian border runs along the foothills of the Ante Lebanon range, the two checkpoints separated by four miles of desolate wasteland. It was here in 1921 that General Gouraud destroyed the Arab army under Emir Faisal, Lawrence's friend and leader of the Arab Revolt, and took Damascus. I wasn't planning anything so dramatic. All I wanted was a cheap hotel so my backpack and I could recover.

Gouraud didn't have to worry about passport control. I did. Fortunately my driver took charge: "Give me passport and follow me." He chatted rapidly with many officials and then gestured for me to step forward. "Business or pleasure?" inquired the mistrustful head official. I felt like saying, "Neither," but this wasn't the time for sarcasm. "Pleasure," I replied. He raised his eyebrows as if he found it hard to believe that anyone would undertake such a journey for fun. One hour later, pale and exhausted, I was in Damascus. I thanked my driver for the lifetime flashbacks but he didn't understand, so we both smiled and waved goodbye.

The hotel recommended by anyone who had an opinion was either Funduq Alrabie or Al Rabi or Alarabia, depending on whose spelling you believed. It was on the southern side of Martyrs' Square. The driver found the square all right but had never, in his entire Damascus taxi-driving career, heard of anything close to Alrabie.

"Alrabie?"

"Yes, its near Martyrs' Square."

"Yes, we are here. This is the square but I live here all my life and I never hear of Alribi."

"No. Alrabie."

"I know a good hotel."

"No thanks."

After much circling we stopped to ask a kebab-maker and he pointed up a dimly-lit street to a sign saying Hotel El Arabia. Close enough, I thought.

The hotelier spoke no English and seemed totally unimpressed with my arrival. He rang a bell, returned to his seat and lit a cigarette. An adolescent with one of those 'need-to-wait-another-year' moustaches arrived and ushered me into a shabby lift. My fifth floor room was only marginally more comfortable than a bus station bench and the plumbing would have had Amnesty International up in arms. Following the day's theme, the adolescent insisted on trying to communicate with me. After about 20 minutes we managed to establish that I was English.

"Ahh. English. Very good. London? Yes, good. You have fun?"

"Loads thanks."

"Chmidim?"

"Sorry?"

"Chmidim?"

"I'm sorry. I don't understand. English."

"Yes. English. Chmidim?"

I was too tired to deal with this so I tried to shove him out of the room. Taking this as a sign of friendliness, he became more persistent.

"Chmidim, midim."

I nodded as convincingly as possible, thinking that "Chmidim" meant something like, "Are you here on vacation?"

He left, only to return moments later with a large woman who was once just unattractive, but had since deteriorated with age. She presented herself in a clashing array of brightly-coloured underwear and leered at me without a full quota of teeth. The penny dropped and I suppressed a yelp of horror. With a wide variety of frantic gestures I explained that this was all a terrible misunderstanding and that my wife and seven children back home would be very upset. The pimp and the prostitute eventually took my behaviour as a sign of madness and left me alone and intact. I bolted the door and left early the next morning to find an Arabic dictionary and the right hotel.

Despite the relatively small distance between the two capitals, the cultural and political differences between Damascus and Beirut are enormous. After the dynamic, forward-thrusting, Western nature of Beirut, I found Damascus more or less the opposite — ancient *souks*, no English, no Western points of reference and the regular call to prayer over the loud-speakers. For several days I wandered in a daze through the overwhelming chaos of the world's oldest city, getting knocked down by bicycles and becoming increasingly blunt with carpet-sellers. The soundtrack of shouting touts and black marketeers, speeding traffic and Islamic incantation from every minaret added to the thrill and exhaustion.

Through old bullet holes in the roof, pin-pricks of sunlight pierced the darkness of the Souk al-Hamidiye. Still in Beirut mode, I assumed the cause of the holes was some violent insurrection or fatal disagreement. I later found out that the blame rested with Bedouins who fired rounds to announce their arrival in the city. I made a mental note not to invite a Bedouin to a dinner party.

Souks are stressful places to negotiate if you're a tourist. Like every other gullible foreigner I ended up in a shop drinking tea with a carpet salesman.

"Welcome London, welcome. Come have tea. You don't have to buy. Just rest and drink."

And after two cups of tea. "For Japanese I ask much dollar. But my nephew live in London. English good people. I give you good price."

Another cup and my point-blank refusal to discuss prices was becoming embarrassing. No matter how many times he said, "Welcome London, welcome," I wasn't going to buy a silver elephant trinket. Eventually, worn down by his expert persistence, I exchanged "dollarie" for a "fine, not rubbish" caftan I knew I would never wear. Once again I was free to wander.

After another 20 minutes of people yelling "Marlboro! Marlboro" or whispering "you got dollar? Good rate" I was in need of refuge. The Souk al-Hamidiye ends beneath a Roman arch. Directly ahead, one of the world's great religious sites offers calm. There could not be a greater contrast between the tranquillity of the Umayyad Mosque and the maelstrom of the *souks* around it. It's easy to see why some Muslims consider it the fourth most holy place after Mecca, Medina and the Dome of the Rock.

The mosque's courtyard is like a small version of Venice's Piazza San Marco, but the marble floor and lack of tourists and postcard-sellers make it feel far bigger. People have worshipped here for the past 3000 years and parts of the existing building date back to the third century BC. Modern life seems to have been left at the gates. Black-gowned women passed in and out of the great arches behind their bead-twiddling husbands. Families rest by central fountains and everyone looks about as relieved as I was to find somewhere calm to pass the time. I returned many times to wander around the Great Mosque in my socks.

Further east along the city walls, the backgammon salesmen and hustlers disappeared and I spent indeterminate hours getting lost in quiet medieval alleyways. Overhanging houses almost touch across the deserted passages, and every time a path looks like a dead end a small archway leads into another street or some uncharted courtyard. Without a doubt, Damascus cartographers have the hardest job in the world.

The tradition of communal bathing continues to conjure its healing and tortuous magic as an antidote to Damascus stress. I discovered this essential part of Middle Eastern travel through a doorway which opened into a beautiful 11th century domed room, beyond which lies a maze of steam rooms and chambers. The staff of the Mouaffak Hammam in Souk al-Bazutiye assumed I knew the ropes. So after stripping down to a rather minimalist towel I found myself wearing shoes where I shouldn't, soaping up in the wrong chamber and almost — though not quite — mistaking the toilet for a wash bowl.

After 20 minutes of lamely wandering around pouring token bowls of water over myself, the staff lost patience. I was told to lie on the marble floor and had what felt like a wire brush applied with skin-removing ferocity. Understanding for the first time how cars must feel in automatic washes, I was shoved semi-conscious and itchy fleshed into a sauna. Before I could call for help, a body-builder type marched me into yet another room and began the massage. A more accurate description would be bodily assault. A near lethal combination of pummelling and karate was eventually concluded with a swift chop to the kidneys and a twist to the neck. I pulled myself together, realigned my limbs and returned to the sauna for solace.

Back in the more civilised domed room I was de-towelled and re-towelled, shown to a comfortable sofa and served sweet tea. This last-minute bit of diplomacy was no doubt intended to dissuade law suits. But as my skin glowed and my vertebrae recovered, the brutality of the previous hour seemed worthwhile. I was ready to get knee-deep in *souks* and bicycles again.

Life, Love and War: A First Journey

by Nicholas Fogg

After the Six Day War of 1967, a mood of anti-Arab hysteria prevailed in Britain, with its usual mass of contradictions. Arabs were cowardly, but always seeking to fight aggressive wars; they were backward and incompetent, but spent millions on the latest military technologies; the Palestinians, who had been driven from their own lands, were likely to sweep the Israelis into the sea.

In the midst of this conflicting propaganda I accepted an official invitation to Jordan. At Amman airport in April, 1970 (our plane had been flown part of the way by the then Crown Prince Hassan), we were greeted by a welcoming delegation and the local press and television. We were then ferried to the Hotel Jordan, where I met Achmet, the barman and an old soldier.

Achmet expressed admiration for the British officers he had served under in the Arab Legion and disappointment that Britain had not supported the Palestinian cause. He lived on the West Bank until he was compelled to leave during the Six-Day War, and had since heard that his old house had been bulldozed to make way for a car park.

Despite his military background and his suffering, Achmet's feelings towards the world remained sanguine. "People", he told us, "laugh at the

Arabs and say we can't make war properly. As though that is a good thing to be able to do. Myself, I want to make love, life, not war."

Next morning an armed escort arrived to take us to the Jordan Valley. It was our first view of this spectacular country and its fierce heat. It was also our first encounter with Arab driving. This was driving purely in the technical sense. Our cars were ridden like unbroken Arab thoroughbreds. The driver had one hand dangling outside the car, the other, holding a cigarette, curved nonchalantly over the wheel. Lorries were overtaken on hairpin bends overlooking 100-feet drops. If he wasn't sure we'd got a particular point he was making, the driver would turn round to explain it.

We soon got used to the incessant blare coming from the radio and found its Arab rhythms absorbing. One singer always produced particular approbation from the driver. He went on to tell us the exotic legends of Um Kaltoom, 'The Voice of God'. She held a diplomatic passport, lived in a palace guarded by troops and was 74. For an hour each day she sang about love and mysticism to all the Arab nations. She aroused deep passion among the common people and our taxi driver told us that if she were ever kidnapped by the Israelis, they would rise to a man and the war would be over in a day.

Um Kaltoom was on the airwaves at a roadside cafe where we stopped for refreshments. As we gulped iced drinks, we felt the immediacy of war when our guide casually mentioned that 18 people had recently been killed at the cafe after Israeli planes dropped two bombs on the wooden building in the belief that it was a commando base. The drink no longer seemed refreshing and we moved on. The object of our trip was the town of Karama in the Jordan Valley, where Palestinian commandos had fought the Israelis to a stand-still.

Modern war has a high media profile. Expecting an easy victory, the Israelis assembled the press corps in Jericho and announced their intention to attack Karama at a specific time. The news leaked through to the beleaguered town. Women and children were evacuated and the commandos massed in the hills. In the fight that followed, the Israelis were held off. With ammunition running low, young boys and old men threw rocks at the enemy. The Jordanian army, which had watched passively, joined in. The Israeli advance was halted, but at a terrible cost. Two years later we stood among the ruins of what had been a prosperous town of 50,000 people. Few remained, so the Israelis had achieved their objective.

Karama was mainly inhabited by beetles and scuttling lizards. Amongst the ruins of what was once a school, exercise books left by fleeing children were scattered on the floor.

Yousef Hafez Salliq, an 18-year old student, was visiting relatives on the day of the battle. He claimed to have taken no part in it, but he was captured and taken across the Jordan. That afternoon we were taken to the King Hussein Bridge, the border with the Occupied Territories, to see him handed back. He was being released because he was suffering from acute asthma. The heat seemed even more intense than before.

We watched an Israeli and a Jordanian officer trying to sort out the individual tragedies of a stream of appellants. An old woman wanted to join her children on the West Bank; a student wished to return to study in Bethlehem, a farmer wanted to take his produce to market in Jericho. The Israeli looked very American in his blue uniform and spoke English with a Brooklyn accent, the Jordanian appeared very British in khaki and black beret, spoke with the accent of someone educated at Sandhurst. They seemed to be men doing a job they didn't want to be doing and we were impressed by the careful humanity with which they considered each case.

Yousef Hafez Salliq arrived on the far side of the bridge in an ambulance. Cruel necessity dictated that he would have to walk the 20 yards to the ambulance waiting on the other side. Two Israeli paramedics virtually carried him halfway and handed him on. Once across, he answered questions through an interpreter. His eyes were blank and his mouth hung open. He said his captors had tortured him by hanging him on a wall in chains for hours.

A few days later we saw him in hospital. He seemed much better and could smile and joke, but his eyes were still glazed. In the next bed another recently-released prisoner would not give us his name or have his picture taken as he still had relatives on the West Bank, but admitted he had been a commando. Both his legs were missing below the knee. He claimed that he was shot in the foot when he was captured and his injury ignored until gangrene set in. When he was taken to hospital, the wrong leg was amputated. The other one was later cut off.

A doctor spoke of a friend who had been captured. He claimed to have been beaten daily as his captors tried to make him confess that he was a commando. "They have invented new tortures," the doctor told us. "My friend had his mouth stuffed with rock salt and was forced to run in the sun at bayonet point while a guard ran in front pouring water on the ground. He was told he could drink when he confessed. Now he is back, but I haven't seen him for six months. I understand he is in a mental hospital."

Everyone seemed to have a story of torture. The Palestinian Red Crescent presented a number of alleged victims to us. Their accounts made for unpleasant listening.

Abdul Hadi Nasr claimed he was asleep at home in Rafah when Israeli soldiers looted his house. His two-year old daughter, lying on the floor, was trampled and later died. He was taken to the Military Governor's office and beaten unconscious. When charges that he was a guerrilla could not be proved, he and his family were told to leave the country. He is now permanently deaf in one ear.

A 20 year-old student, Moayar Otham, was accused of possessing arms and belonging to Al Fatah. He claimed he was hung from a ceiling in a small cellar and beaten until he lost consciousness. His eyes were bandaged and he was forced to run over ground full of holes. Each time he fell he was beaten until he started running again. Electric shocks were administered to his head. He was burnt with cigarettes and hit on the genitals.

Raubi el-Khatib was Mayor of Jerusalem during the Six Day War. He had clung to office for six months until forced to leave. He gave us his account of what happened when the Israelis took over his city. "They started by spreading terror, outside and inside mosques and churches, raiding houses, shops and garages, looting whatever they could lay their hands on, treating cruelly anyone who showed the slightest sign of disaffection. They gathered people from their homes, keeping them standing for hours, irrespective of age or sex and jailing hundreds of people for unlimited periods, in most cases for no reason whatsoever. They were creating waves of terror to force people to leave."

Such stories were universally believed. Even if only a small number were true, then serious crimes had been committed. During our visit a UN team was investigating some of the allegations, but we never heard the outcome.

One witness was an Anglican priest, the Rev. Eli Khoury. After the war he was arrested and kept in solitary confinement for 48 days before being expelled from Palestine. He now was running a mission in the slums of Amman. Funds were low and there were too many needing help. He took in girls from refugee families and, with his small staff, taught them domestic skills, writing and reading.

"These are the mothers of tomorrow," he said. "We teach them the skills and they pass them on, not only to their parents, but to their future children. It's like a snowball."

The PLO's declared ambition was to create a secular state that would encompass all religions. Precedent was sought in the multicultural heritage of the Levant. "We have Muslims and Christians here", a school headmistress told us. "One day there will be Jews."

Topic of the moment was the impending visit to Amman of the US Assistant Secretary of State, Joseph Sisco. The powerful Zionist lobby in the US ensured unrelenting support for Israel, but 'real-politik' meant that strategic and commercial links in the Arab world should be preserved. Jordan, a moderate Arab monarchy, was therefore a key player. Sisco's mission was undermined by the announcement that America was to supply Israel with Phantom jets. On the eve of his arrival, the American Library was burnt down by chanting students. Another mob attacked the embassy, burning three cars and tearing down the flag before running up a Palestinian one.

We watched the riots from our hotel bar. As columns of smoke curled skywards, Achmet interpreted events for the assembled press corps who would pass on his knowledge in the next day's newspapers. Sisco's visit was cancelled.

The next day we went to the headquarters of Al Fatah. We were greeted by Kemal Nasser, an ebullient man who looked incongruous in military fatigues.

"Do you know what religion I am?" he asked.

"Muslim?" I ventured.

"Try again."

"Christian?"

"Yes", he roared. "Church of England!"

The curiosities thrown up by Britain's imperial past never fail to amaze me. He offered no explanation of this extra-ordinary affiliation and I wondered whether the Archbishop of Canterbury was aware of this most exotic of his flock.

"Our enemy is Zionism," he declared, "and Zionism is hated even by many Jews themselves. The Zionists are expansionists. What they are after is territory. Always more territory. Eventually they must overreach themselves and then they will have lost.

"I hope they capture Baghdad. That's the secret, extend them beyond what they can control and they will fall apart. There will never be a peaceful political settlement. There is too much hatred.

"Europeans have a collective guilt over what happened to the Jews in the war. They have the impression of a brave little country defending itself against the might of Arab armies. They forget that this brave little country has displaced millions of peaceful Arabs from Palestine – people who only wanted to live in their homes and wanted nothing of war."

Kemal pointed out that the Palestinian refugees were descendants of peoples who had lived there for thousands of years. That Kemal was a poet of some distinction was evident in his use of language.

"There will be a bloodbath very soon," he continued. "There will be no victor except the man who sits on his horse at the end of the fight and then collapses."

I recalled these words some months later when Israeli commandos raided his apartment in Beirut. His blood-stained corpse was pictured in the papers.

Bidding farewell to this friendly pessimist, we took a short cut to our hotel across the valley. We passed a group of Bedouin soldiers of the Arab Legion laying a barbed wire blockade across the approach road to the American Embassy. One sensed they would not hesitate to fire on a crowd if so ordered. Their ability to mutely convey this made it unlikely that anyone would push them that far. I suddenly realised that the Palestinians were on the verge of disaster. These troops were disciplined, tough and entirely loyal to the King. The PLO was becoming a state within a state. The events of the day before represented a challenge no authority could permit and then survive.

Our way lay across scrubland. We were halfway across the valley when the first stone landed at our feet. We realised that our route led towards the American Embassy. At first there were only three children, then six, then a dozen. Shouting "Sisco", they bombarded us with rocks the size of oranges. In a pincer movement, another bombardment began from rooftops across the road. Wishing to identify ourselves as friendly, we shouted "Al Fatah" and made a victory sign. The barrage lessened and then resumed. We debated doing a pre-emptive charge, but thought that this might land us in greater trouble. We dashed into a shop doorway before a man appeared and spoke to the kids. They put down their rocks and ambled off. He waved and followed them. We never discovered who he was.

Some days later we were taken into the Jordan valley to meet an Al Fatah commando unit. The sudden lushness of the river banks provided a vivid contrast to the arid road out of Amman. Signs of fighting were everywhere. The twisted remains of an aircraft had its Royal Jordanian Airforce insignia still visible. We were met by a jeep with a powerful machine gun trained nervously skywards. Its presence did not reassure me. It would have been observed on the other side of the river and might provoke an attack.

We were dropped on the edge of the undergrowth and led through dense and exotic foliage. After about 100 yards we came to a clearing with a shack in it. Squatting on the ground was a unit of 11 *fedayhin*. The youngest was just 17. He handled his machine gun, captured from the Israelis, as if it was an extra limb. He spoke excellent English, in accents that seemed familiar. He revealed he was from Birmingham and had joined Al Fatah after hearing about it at his mosque. No names were given and none were asked. Most of the men had relatives in the occupied territories and our cameras caused some concern. We tactfully put them away.

Apart from their identities, they had nothing to hide. "We don't look to the West for arms" their leader declared. "All we want is for people to know the truth. We don't want to expand. We're fighting to get back the homes which have been taken from us."

They claimed to have recently killed 20 Israelis who were preparing to ambush them. "After that," said one, "they announced just three casualties, but I killed more than that myself. They were all dead."

"They are cowards," said another. "They rarely venture from their well prepared positions. They recently installed surveillance equipment along the west bank of the Jordan River, so we ceased our normal operations for a while and spent our time destroying it."

Operating so close to the river they had been caught in the cross-fire that occasionally opened up. They confessed that it was only a matter of time before the Israelis discovered their whereabouts. Then they would move on.

We shared their meal of fish and fruit. Apart from our murmured conversation, the only sound was the lazy hum of the flies. Then one said; "The air attacks come without warning. The pilots cut out their engines so you can't hear them coming, drop their bombs and then go back for more." We searched the sky nervously for signs of silent planes.

We bade our farewells and I have often wondered what became of those men. For all the violence they embodied, they seemed to represent a new way forward, an idealistic regeneration of the Palestinian people. But a lot has happened since then, and this idealism has not fulfilled what, seemed in those heady days, to be its limitless potential.

There were an estimated one million refugees in Jordan. At one camp we saw the cause of the anger that fuelled the guerrilla movement. It housed 15,000 people in huts the size of pigeon lofts and was extremely squalid. Funnily enough, I never managed to take a picture of a refugee camp that didn't come out looking like a Club Med resort. It must have been the combination of sun, sand, huts and palms. We went with our usual trepidation. The Ministry of Information warned us not to go. "The last time I took round a party we were shot at," advised one official. "They don't like being looked on as animals in a zoo." We put our faith in Al Fatah's power in the camps and in the armed guard provided for us.

In a tiny wooden hut we met a mother and her four children. They slept on threadbare rugs on a stone floor. The only furniture was a chair, a table and a portable radio, but hand-sewn curtains covered the glassless windows and it was spotlessly clean. All her washing and cooking was done outside, but even that was a luxury for most of the inhabitants. The woman's husband had been a commando. Before he had been forced to flee from the West Bank he had been a hard-working provider for his family. "He didn't want to fight," she told us through an interpreter. "All he wanted was his home back. Now he is dead."

The next day our tour entered a new dimension. The road south from Amman is now on the tourist circuit. Then it was remote and exuded a feeling of danger, with frequent roadblocks manned by troops. Our drivers were skilled at shouting at the right pitch to get through Just enough to create nervousness about the potential consequences of hindering our progress. This was the part of our itinerary the Jordanian government most wanted us to see — the real Arab lands, unsullied by the debris of rapid progress and war.

One's first view of the desert is breathtaking and intriguing. In those days you could drive for an hour without seeing anything but rock, sand and an occasional truck trundling in the opposite direction. It was the sight of a Bedouin sitting by the side of the road that made us realise that the landscape, seemingly barren, was full of life. He didn't want a lift, he just wanted to sit there. Herds of camels held up the car as they crossed the road with scornful dignity. We saw a woman in the distance, carrying a kitchen table on her head, her destination a mystery.

Our first stop was the 'rose red city' of Petra. Although I am always spellbound whenever I return there, nothing can compare with this first visit. Staying the night in the tourist lodge, we woke early and took a buggy through the narrow Wadi as-Sik. The experience was as close as one could get to that of John Lewis Burckhardt when he rediscovered the city that had existed in legend for 1000 years. It was empty and we wandered undisturbed all day

At Aqaba we surveyed the scene from the balcony of our seaside hotel. "Down there are our good neighbours," our guide explained. Our eyes followed the wave of his arm. It was the only place in the world where a beach was divided between hostile factions. Beyond the barbed wire entanglements lay the Israeli port of Eilat. Access to the Red Sea was so valuable to both sides, that an uneasy truce prevailed. It had been jeopardised recently when six Palestinian frogmen swum over and blew up a bridge. Reprisals could come any day. The conflict bore in on us again.

We walked the 100 yards to inspect it. The people on the other side were doing what people do on beaches — swimming, sunbathing, and snogging. Some responded to our waves. The war retreated. Returning, we were accosted by a tall willowy man in Arab gear. I took him for a deckchair attendant, but it was explained that he was a Saudi prince who was inviting us to his seaside villa that evening. When we arrived, a bottle of whisky was produced and we sat in a circle on the floor to drink it. First ourselves, then the Prince.

His Royal Highness was a poet and sang one of his haunting songs. It told of the parting of lovers. He described his love's hair, her waist, her flaming eyes and her eyebrows, black as a raven's wing. Then he asked us to sing a song. After hasty discussion, the two Yorkshiremen in our party suggested On Ilkley Moor Baht'at. The Prince was charmed by the words and we discussed their meaning. The bottle of whisky was duly replaced, and as the evening mellowed, I admired the Prince's flowing robes. He snapped his fingers. A servant took me to an ante-room and fitted me with an identical costume. There was no question of giving it back. I had a vision of returning with all his riches in my suitcase and refrained from admiring anything else. A return gift seemed appropriate, so the Prince became the proud owner of a British Home Stores sweater.

On our way back to Amman two days later, our driver spied a Bedouin camp of long, low black tents near the desert city of Ma'an. He decided we should visit Sheikh Feisal Ben Jazi. In the largest tent we sat on luxurious carpets and were served coffee from an exotic curved pot. Our cups were replenished at every sip. We waited in silence for the Sheikh to appear, until we were told quietly by our driver that he was seated with the other Bedouin to our right and would like to talk to us. He spoke of Lawrence of Arabia, an old comrade of his father. Like everyone else, he admired Britain and was disappointed we had done so little to alleviate a situation that was of our creation.

From Amman, we flew to Beirut. It was clear that this beautiful, cosmopolitan city was on a cusp. The Palestinian refugees represented an additional force in a country of fine balances. Many Lebanese resented their presence. "How can you show sympathy for strangers?" was a common reaction. There was much talk of Israel's intention to destabilise Southern Lebanon. The first attacks came before my second visit and set in motion the tragedy of this beautiful country, part of the continuing tragedy for the Palestinians.

* * * * *

I have returned to the Middle East frequently and worked on programmes which helped advance the peace processes. I have amended my first impressions, realising that there are enlightened and progressive Israelis who deeply desire peace and justice. Yet the tragedy of the Palestinians seems to take on a new dimension with each generation. The prediction of a West Bank professor still haunts me: "When there is a settlement, the leadership in exile will return and constitute an elite over those who stayed and suffered."

The idealism of 1970 remains a dream, but the prognosis is not entirely gloomy. At the first seminars on the issue at Harvard, it was an achievement to get Palestinians and Israelis in the same building, let alone the same room. The gain of the peace process is the chance for objectivity, to separate truth from rhetoric and to hope that the tragedy will be lessened by the healing process of time.

From Debka to Break Dancing

by Sejal Mandalia

"Does everyone stare at you all the time?" asked 19-year-old Jamal. With large blue eyes, blond hair that was slicked back and shaved on all sides and 'crotch-at-knee-level' combat trousers, Jamal would have looked more at home in a teenage boy-band, than in the Gaza Strip. His blond hair came from his Irish-American mother. He was in Gaza because his Palestinian father had decided it was about time his son learnt about his Palestinian roots. Although Jamal's father had lived in New York for more than 20 years, his uncles had remained in Gaza. Originally from Majdal (now known as Ashkelon), their family were forced out of their home town by Israeli military forces in 1948.

After being born and raised in New York, Jamal was finding life in closed and conservative Gaza a shock to his system.

"I'm enjoying my Arabic classes which are two hours a day, but apart from that, life here sucks. There's nothing to do, it is so boring," he moaned. "At least I've got Ashour here to hang out with. He's the only one who understands how I feel."

Ashour strutted towards us. With his dark features, the only thing that gave away his American upbringing were his baggy jeans, puffer jacket and trainers. The same age as Jamal, he was arrived in Gaza nine months earlier.

"Does everyone stare at you on the streets?" he asked me in his thick New Jersey accent. Both were suffering from a severe complex. In a society that was traditional and Islamic, and where New York fashion was not exactly thriving, they were very conspicuous.

I asked, what life in Gaza was like, apart from the stares?

"Well for the first four months, I thought I was going mad," said Ashour. "There's nothing fun to do in Gaza. Having lived in America all my life where people have boyfriends and girlfriends, and go clubbing all the time, I find it very closed here. A few months ago I managed to get a job as a translator with (Yasser) Arafat's Dahar company which pays well, so I don't mind being here as much as I used to. Eventually you get used to Gaza."

"Yeah," added Jamal, "that's true, but I just wish it wasn't so difficult to meet girls."

It's easy to understand Jamal and Ashour's claustrophobia. Entering Gaza from Israel is a culture shock. On the drive from the Erez checkpoint at the Israeli border you are surrounded by a mass of grey concrete on both sides. It's hard to tell when the sprawling bulk of Jabalia, one of the largest Palestinian refugee camps, ends and when the looming towers of Gaza City begin. In this tiny strip of land, 40 kilometres long and in some areas only six kilometres wide, more than one million Palestinians and around 5000 Jewish settlers rub shoulders. No wonder it feels as if they are living in a human pressure cooker.

There is no greenery in sight as dusty roads offset the even dirtier grey-brown houses that line the streets. Since there is not much room to expand outwards, the houses in Gaza expand up. Since the Palestinian Authority (PA) took over municipal control of Gaza in 1994, there has been a boom in construction as Palestinian businessmen deemed it to be the only safe investment in the politically unstable climate. It was also ripe for investment after almost 30 years of neglect, when Palestinians were routinely denied building permits during the Israeli military occupation.

Wandering through the sand swept streets of Gaza City, it is the quiet pervading peace that is most startling. Gaza seems to be in a perpetual slumber. At the city's main seafront, where the five-star hotels lie, the Palestinian soldiers lounge about at checkpoints, staring as I passed, their guns nowhere in sight. Men sit gossiping on chairs outside their customer-free shops.

It's hard to believe that these people managed to do what the combined might of the state armies of the Arab world failed to, convince the all-conquering Israeli Defence Forces to leave their camps and towns. The images of violence and anarchy which so epitomised Gaza during the years of the *Intifada* (the Palestinian Uprising), from 1987 to 1993, seem incomprehensible in Gaza today.

Yet there were two consequences of the peace process that Gaza's inhabitants seemed totally unprepared for — the influx of Palestinian returnees, and more importantly, their social and economic impact on the Palestinian territories.

I met Jamal and Ashour at a birthday party held in an apartment in Rimal, an expensive neighbourhood in Gaza City where Yasser Arafat lived, and where most of the PA's most important ministries were located. The party was a strange mixture of foreign staff working for the numerous non-governmental organisations that had recently sprung up in Gaza, and Palestinian returnees.

After the signing of the 1993 Peace Accord between Israel and the PLO in Oslo, many Palestinians who had been living in exile in the Arab world or as far afield as Canada, returned to the West Bank and Gaza. Locals scornfully refer to them as 'Tunisians' since Tunis was the PLO's base prior to Gaza and because of the 'modern' habits they picked up in countries more liberal than Gaza. Habits they had no qualms flaunting in public, no matter how much it irked the Islamic sensitivities of the average non-returnee Palestinian. As a general rule of thumb, you could spot a 'returnee' because the women would be hijab-less (veil-less) and wearing designer clothes, often short sleeved, and the men would be drinking whisky and smoking cigars.

This was certainly the case at the party where the ratio of men to women was about 10 to one. Palestinian men, I was told, had not yet caught on to the idea of socialising with their wives. The young men, all dressed in jeans and shirts, crammed into the kitchen relishing the rare opportunity in Gaza to drink vast quantities of alcohol. Their alcoholic banter was conducted in French, rather than Arabic.

Ray, a UN veteran from Ireland who had worked in Palestine since 1986, noticed my bemused expression, and explained: "It's very difficult for people here to get access to alcohol, so when they do, they tend to go mad and drink till they collapse."

The merriment was briefly halted when the landlord found out about the party and ordered that everyone leave.

"Why has he ordered us to leave?" I asked Tahir, a Palestinian friend.

"Because there's alot of *shebab* (young men) here and he thinks they'll get very drunk and sleep around with the foreign girls," he answered.

"But there are hardly any women here. There's about one to every 20 guys."

"Yes," smiled Tahir, "that would be very tiring for them."

Leaving the building we passed Abu Jessel, the landlord, and his four sons sitting outside on guard duty, making sure we had gone.

Still perplexed by what seemed to be an unjustifiably puritanical reaction, I looked to Ray for an answer.

"Everyone here is obsessed with sex. It isn't possible for them to believe that men and women can be friends without anything sexual going on," he explained.

It was quickly decided that the Red Cross centre would be the new party venue. The centre looked more like a living room, with comfortable sofas and matching lampshades, rather than an office. Algerian music was swiftly put on, the sofas moved back, and the foot-stomping *debka*, the Palestinian folk dance, began. The men on the dance floor were soon joined by two Australian girls and a Palestinian woman. They formed a line and were hopping around the room, oblivious to everyone else.

Bewildered and sober, I sat on the sofa staring at the scene in front of me. I was seeing a side of Gaza I had been completely unaware of. After spending five weeks teaching in the Al-Shati refugee camp, just outside Gaza city, where the girls asked why I wasn't wearing a *hijab* and the boys asked if I drank whisky so they could find out if I was immoral, the scenes unfolding before me seemed oddly out of place. Yet these returnees, who until a few years ago had been living in much more Westernised societies, saw nothing wrong in their behaviour.

The music suddenly changed. During a respite in the dancing, Jamal and Ashour had seized the opportunity to put on their hip-hop CD. A thin, toothy man, with beady eyes and spectacles sat beside me and asked where I was from.

"I'm from London."

"But you don't look English. You look Indian," he replied.

"Well I live in London, but I'm of Indian-origin."

"But what do you feel? Indian or British?"

These were questions I was constantly being asked by Palestinians. Was it a reflection of their own sense of displacement and national insecurity? The questions, however, unnerved me and prompted my own questions about where I felt I ultimately belonged.

Many of those at the party had been living in different countries before eventually ending up in the Gaza Strip. Labelling themselves 'Palestinians' rather than 'Arabs' was a way of reinforcing the fact that they are a separate nation, a nation that did not disappear with the creation of Israel in 1948. Ashour, for example, told me that when anyone asked where he was from he always said Palestine rather than America.

After years in exile many had built up glorified dreams of their homeland, only to be disillusioned when they returned to the bleak, ultra-conservative Gaza. Marwan Kanafani, Arafat's spokesperson, best summed up the mood of most returnees who arrived in Gaza.

"My family left Jaffa and went to Lebanon in 1948. I had never been to the West Bank or the Gaza Strip before. Working and living in Egypt, Syria, Lebanon and the US, I never had a concept of a homeland as it really is. My concept of a homeland was how I dreamt it to be — full of greenery and wealthy people. So I when I came to Gaza my dreams were shattered. However, like a mother who expects a perfect baby, and then delivers a handicapped son, the child still remains your son and you love it as such. My feelings for Gaza are the same. Even though it is not what I expected, it is still my homeland, and the days I have spent here have been the happiest in my life."

Marwan's sentiments are shared by many others. While some returnees moan and complain about their life in Gaza, others have poured their hearts and money into turning their homeland in to a success.

For anyone who doubted that Gaza was capable of developing into a colourful, thriving, modern city, a visit to the Omar al-Mukhtar street is required. In Rimal's main shopping district, under a beaming portrait of Yasser Arafat, is a huge beautiful park, whose pathways are lined with clipped symmetrical trees, flower beds and the odd brightly coloured billboard urging people to 'Keep Gaza Tidy'. By day youths sit idly on the park benches watching the traffic pass. At night the park becomes a favourite with families who sit on the outside walls devouring the fluorescent pink and yellow ice cream that seems to be so popular with Gazans.

At the far end of the park was perhaps the most blatant sign that Western consumer culture had reached the heart of Gaza — a large pizza restaurant. It was actually called 'Pizza Inn', but the red and white logo was identical to the Pizza Hut chain. On the right side of the road there was a bright neon sign for 'Pizzaland' with a similarly lit up 'Burgerland' next door. A giant Coca Cola bottle-top separated the two. Further down the street you could find small 'designer' boutiques whose clothes even met the approval of New York hipster Jamal. After the clothes shops came the camera shops with huge Fuji and Kodak logos on the shop fronts and various portraits of the owner in different poses on the walls inside.

I went back to Pizzaland. Samir, the owner, opened Pizzaland in 1997, two years after returning to Gaza. He had spent years working in Greece, where he met his wife Jackie, and then Scotland before returning to Gaza.

When I'd met Jackie on my last visit to Gaza, she was finding life in the Strip very difficult to adjust to, and was regretting her decision to leave Scotland with their 10-year-old daughter Nancy. I asked Samir how she was.

"Yes she's still here," said Samir proudly. "Come next door she's there with Nancy." Next door meant Burgerland, so Samir was doing well. In less than a year he had already opened up another fast-food restaurant.

Burgerland seemed to be a favourite hangout for Gaza's teenagers. Groups of girls sat around small tables with red and blue chequered tablecloths, munching burgers and sipping Pepsi. Some wore *hijabs*, but they were all heavily made up and dressed in jeans and platform sandals. A few young men in blazers sat at another table talking intensely about office politics over tiny cups of Arabic coffee. Jackie, came out from the back of the restaurant looking much happier than the last time I saw her.

"Hi, fancy seeing you here again," she said in her soft Scottish accent.

I remarked on how surprised I was to see her still in Gaza.

"Well its not so bad now. I've made friends with some other British women out here who are also married to Palestinians. We keep each other company. Also, Nancy is happy in her new school and I've got a part-time job which I enjoy. Yeah its not so bad here. Oh, by the way, I'm pregnant again."

As we talked, Khalid, the waiter, appeared with glasses of mint tea. With his slicked back dark hair, tight white T-shirt and blue jeans, he looked like he'd just stepped out of a Levi's advert.

Jackie must have noticed why I was suddenly so distracted. "The reason why we get so many girls coming in here is because of Khalid. They all come to see him. At night he and his brother, who works next door, spend hours at the phone booth outside calling all their girlfriends. A few years ago this kind of thing would not be going on. I tell you Gaza is changing, it may be slowly, but its happening."

A visit to Rimal leaves you feeling that things are up and running in Gaza. But just five minutes walk away and you are suddenly made to realise that, maybe, things haven't really progressed that much at all.

A short walk west along the Rimal seafront is the Al-Shati refugee camp, a series of bleak, grey-black buildings made from concrete and corrugated iron which look as if they are about to collapse. As you enter the camp a pathway leads to a maze of one storey high concrete shacks. Some have falling walls, others have newly built floors added to them. Outside the road is littered with household rubbish. Sand whirled around in the breeze, making the streets look even dirtier. Small children wearing brightly coloured jumpers and trousers they outgrew long ago play barefoot in the squalid sand, oblivious to the green trickle of sewage nearby. Approaching the *souk*, high brownish-grey walls line the street. Posters of martyred young men, some fresh-faced, some with full beards, are painted on the walls. Sometimes a picture of the Dome of the Rock can be found in the background, symbolising the ultimate goal of the martyr — to liberate Islam's third holiest site from Israeli control.

More than 70 per cent of Gaza's population are refugees (over 800,000 people). They are descendants of the 200,000 Palestinians who fled from villages in what is now Israel after 1948. The Al-Shati camp, with an area of around one square mile and a population of more than 60,000 people, is one of poorest camps in Gaza after Jabalia and Rafah.

I was in the camp to visit Dalia for lunch. She had been one of my students the year before, and remembering my fondness for *maqlooba*, a Palestinian dish of chicken and spicy vegetable rice, had invited me to her house to sample her mother's cooking.

There was something about Dalia that made her stand-out from the rest of the girls. Tall, with big brown eyes that smiled constantly at you and waist-length dark hair, there was a freshness and energy about her that other girls lacked. Maybe it was her courage to walk around the camp unveiled, her long hair flowing, and wearing body hugging shiny lycra leggings that made her seem so different. Maybe it was the fact that during presentation day at the end of summer camp, while the other girls had their mothers and younger siblings present, Dalia had a group of six teenage boys come to see her. It was only when I met her parents that I understood why she was so remarkable.

Her parents, Hanada and Wael, met at her grandparents' house. Wael used to come and visit his sister who married Hanada's brother. That was when he first saw Hanada. They fell in love. After they got married they stayed at Wael's fathers house with his six brothers, seven sisters and their families. Eventually each sibling left the parental home for their own. Wael was a journalist working for a local newspaper. Hanada wanted to be a doctor, but her family had no money to fund her studies so she ended up working as a nurse at the Shifa hospital. Almost six foot tall with jet black hair and eyes made even larger by *kohl*, Hanada spoke in a voice filled with regret of the day she had to stop working to look after her five children, of whom Dalia, aged 14, was the oldest.

"I want to be a doctor," said Dalia, hoping to accomplish her mother's failed ambition. "But there is a big problem, nobody has money. My father earns 150 shekels a day. It is nothing. If I want to study I need to a lot of money. I have a cousin, she is 27. She finished university for three years and she didn't have work until now. She got a job at a newspaper but that stopped after a month. They wrote about the police, so the police closed it. I see on TV how Israelis say what they want, but here people can't say what they want. Our neighbours know everything about us, and we know everything about them."

"What do the people in the camps think of the Palestinan Authority?" I asked.

"People are scared of the PA. Maybe it's because of Israel. When I was six and my brother was five the Israelis hurt him and took him away, but my mother chased them and got him back. It was very bad. A family next door, one of their sons who was 17 was killed. But now the PA have guns as well," she replied.

Our conversation was interrupted by the arrival of her father. Wael had the same bright, warm eyes as Dalia. The two of them began teasing each other in Arabic. You could tell they were very close.

"I love my father. He speaks to me like a friend, not just a daughter," gushed Dalia.

Dalia's mother brought in a huge tray of *maqlooba* and accompanying bowls of salad. Dalia's younger brothers, their mischievous eyes flashing shyly at the stranger in their home, sat beside their mother. Soon everyone was eating from the communal plate.

From the outside all you could see of the homes in the camp were the tall brownish-grey walls which made one home so indistinguishable from the other. Yet if you entered through any of the gates, you would often find a brightly decorated and spotlessly clean interior. The small courtyard in Dalia's home was painted white with a border of red flowers running along the top of the white-washed walls. Inside the front room, large framed pictures of family members were hung up and, as in most Muslim homes, so was a gold-plated print of the Dome of the Rock.

I asked Dalia what she did in her spare time.

"I go and play with my cousins. Sometimes on Friday my father takes us to Dier al Balah or Rafah. Sometimes we go to Shalihat."

I was surprised that her family went to Shalihat, the very up market beach club just down the road from Arafats's Presidential Office. It was a popular haunt for those working with the PA and their families, as well as other returnees. It was also one of the very few places in Gaza where it was acceptable for women not to have to swim fully clothed. As such, it was scorned as a place of sin by many camp residents.

"Shalihat made me feel uncomfortable," said Dalia. "There's a big difference between them and us. I see boys and girls with each other, speaking and touching, but if I do that then people around me would think I am bad. Sometimes I wish I was a boy so I could go out and run and play."

After lunch and tea it was time for me to go. I hugged Dalia's mother goodbye and shook hands with her father. "Come back again. You are most welcome," said Hanada. Dalia and her younger brothers walked with me to the edge of the camp.

We passed the local *souk* with wooden stalls squeezed together and overloaded with vegetables and fruit, the spillage lying trampled on the ground with the rest of the market refuge. Small boys riding rickety old donkey carts passed in the main passage way, waving sticks and shouting to their friends. In the midst of all the chaos I noticed a recent addition. A brand new, concrete market was being built courtesy of the PA and European donors.

Physical changes in the camp were starting to show as a result of the Peace Process. Yet for the Palestinians who sacrificed so much during the Intifada for their freedom, a new market did not necessarily bring about a new world.

The Last Resort

by Amar Grover

"Now, how do we get in?" he asked mischievously. Before our faces dangled a peculiar key resembling a fat elongated toothbrush with pins instead of bristles, yet there was no obvious lock or keyhole. Ali Bouzed grinned. As 'le gardien' this was his responsibility and he was savouring the moment. Thrusting the key through a small gap by the door jam, he pushed it home behind the door panels. As the pins clicked into the sockets, he yanked a wooden bar and the door creaked open. We were through into Amtoudi's *agadir* or fortress granary — one of the finest in all Morocco.

Stooping, Ali Bouzed led us through a steep, dark passageway. Shafts of light lit up the earth floor like spotlights at the theatre. Suddenly we emerged onto an open bluff where warrens of dilapidated chambers and cells threaded past boulders and overhangs. Palm ladders with steps grooved into single trunks offered access to about 70 cubicles and there were remains of cisterns and water channels. "And what do you think of these?" he asked, pointing to skeletal and enigmatic grids of slate. An armoury? An aviary? I shrugged. "For honey," he enthused, but the honey bees are long gone from these hives.

Earlier, the morning sun had yet to warm the Boulgous Canyon's floor as we filed through Amtoudi village. Women and children shepherded sheep and goats up flinty paths that weaved high above flat-roofed houses and faded amidst cliffs and scree. Climbing these barren southern flanks of the Ante Atlas range, we looked down on olive groves, almond trees and date palms. Rough stone walls separated brown and green, desert from life.

With its turrets and crenellations, our goal seemed grafted onto the steep bluff. Ali Bouzed, our guide, urged us through several small ruined gateways until we stood beneath sheer stone walls that curved artfully around the crown of the hill. Before us was a coarse wooden door, mottled and dimpled from age, wind and sun. It held firm to our push — until the cheeky Ali Bouzed produced his unique entry pass.

It is not known exactly when Amtoudi ceased to be a working agadir, but it is believed to be about 40 or 50 years ago. Ali put its age at 1000 years, but a few hundred is more likely. Even as we poked about like children, his eyes inspected every nook and cranny, fingers prodding here and there. He assumed the role of guardian after his father died and he has the only entry key.

"When it needs work, I ask around the village. Our boys usually help," he told me.

We lingered in this stirring place and watched as the first rays of sun baked the landscape. In the distance you could clearly see the Boulgous river draining into the empty desert.

About two kilometres further up the Boulgous stands Agadir Agalouil, our next target. We strolled through the ribbon of palms and greenery that seemed to twitch with every sound and movement by the flocks of tiny birds. Women with scythes and baskets crouched in fields of potato and barley, their men chatting languidly in the shade. Emerging onto the bleached watercourse, we caught a glimpse of Agadir Agalouil through a gap in the trees. Perched heroically on a shaft of rock, this agadir was even more striking than the first.

The men warned us against venturing inside, but we were rash enough to ignore them. Crouching in the watchtower and peering through holes with dizzying views of the gorge below, one felt the whole thing might suddenly slide off the precipice. Though its walls had not been breached and were intact, the passageways were filled with debris. Beams had collapsed along with parts of the roof. Broken doors hung from the densely arranged cells, while shards of pottery and even the odd shoe lay scattered about. Fleeing here to hole up for days or weeks, cramped and uncomfortable, must clearly have been a last desperate resort. Here is the *agadir* of last resort and Agadir the tourist resort. They couldn't possibly be more disparate, yet confusion between the two became a rich seam of amusement during surreal exchanges with bemused locals.

"I would like to see the *agadir*, please tell me where it is?"

"*Mais monsieur, c'est loin*, it's far..." they would reply.

"But I like walking your mountains, the scenery..."

"You are lost, *monsieur*, it's very far, it's hot and you have a car. I don't understand this walking..." and they would gesture back the way we'd come and beyond to Tiznit or Taroudannt until it was clear they had Agadir, 100 or so kilometres away, in mind. With its beach, bikinis and bars, this was the only possible Agadir for Westerners.

The *agadir* can be found all across the Maghreb, but the most developed ones are in Morocco. They were built by mountain Berbers to store and protect their grain, oil and seeds, sometimes even their animals. Having the granaries ensured a steady supply of food when crops failed or supplies ran low. They also keep the food safe from thieves. In times of unrest, when tribal and clan conflicts pitted one valley tribe against another, they became bolt holes so entire communities could take refuge. It was a feudal age, best summed up by The Times' correspondent, Walter Harris, in 1921: "Every tribe had its enemies, every family had its blood-feuds, and every man his would-be murderer."

For centuries Morocco had known a distinct division between the Bled el Makhzen — the land of government — and Bled es Siba, the land of 'insolence' or 'anarchy'. Sultans ruled and misruled from the cities of Fez and Marrakesh, while in the hills and valleys, tribal relations with the Sultans remained volatile. According to Harris, the Sultan frequently scoured the country with a huge, unruly entourage. Their "ravages resembled those of a flight of locusts" he wrote, and the Berbers often fled rather than provide food or pay bribes.

Many granaries came to symbolise the Berbers' proud independence. Their catchments were like little republics whose allegiances resembled shifting sands. With the French Protectorate's pacification of most of the country by the 1930s, communities lived more harmoniously than before. Some traditions weakened, the economy developed and the need for fortress granaries diminished. It was not the start of their deterioration. Those few that remain, often in remote and spectacular locations, are compelling reminders of those wilder, tougher times.

My obscure interest in the granaries took some explaining, but rural Berbers are generally friendly rather than suspicious and I needed help. The French word for granary, *granier*, sometimes did the trick, but there are other Berber words for it. In much of the High Atlas it is called an 'igherm' or, if built for a few families, a 'tighremt'.

In Amtoudi we shared a house for the night with some Belgians and over dinner I chatted with their guide, Sabir. His group had hired two landrovers for *le grand tour* and they were heading for Tafraoute, the most visited part of the Ante-Atlas. It's a region of starkly beautiful landscapes — cliffs, plateaux and palm-choked gorges — with a sprinkling of villages. Tafraoute is famed for almonds and the bizarre boulder-strewn scenery that surrounds it. It looks as the Gods once flung down their toys in bad mood..

Although we were planning on heading there as well, Sabir managed to coax us into going with him. Moroccan roads are all ruts, jolts and bumps. To make matters worse Sabir had a four wheel drive and was planning a short cut.

"What about our poor little Renault 4 with its skinny tyres and thin transmission?" I asked.

"No problem, *inshallah*, God willing," he beamed. His faith was touching, but what really sold us was the mention of a ruined agadir, hidden somewhere up in the hills.

What began as a wide, dirt road became a track, then a trail and finally something which had us coaxing the car as if it were a plucky horse. We stopped in a little bit of nowhere called Tarqa Khdayr, a village without men where timid women covered their faces or averted their gaze. The Ante-Atlas, Tafraoute in particular, has a huge emigrant workforce scattered across Morocco. The land is poor and life is grim, without their urban pay packets the families would struggle to survive.

A few kilometres down the road a tell-tale watchtower pinpointed the remote, dilapidated agadir that hugged the cusp of a ridge. It was difficult to imagine a more desolate place. Exposed scree swirled across barren hills. Even the gullies were shrubless. But this little eyrie had once been a sanctuary, the focus of villagers' lives. I scrambled to the foot of its walls, where chambers and hives clung to the precipice like swallows' nests. Though tantalisingly close, the structure remained inaccessible to all but the most serious climber.

It was in the Ante-Atlas that the *agadir* reached its zenith in capacity and sophistication. Families who built them, their ancestors or merchants who paid for the privilege, often had two or three cells at their disposal. Four or five storeys were not uncommon and some had a mosque and meeting room. While few remain intact, even fewer still function with anything like their original purpose.

Tasguent, about 65 kilometres from Tafraoute is exceptional. From afar it resembled an undistinguished blob on top of a grassy knoll. Some young village boys led us towards the agadir along a path that ran through soft, rolling hills. Passing through an open gate, we were left stunned by the sight in front of us. The precise, almost mosaic, stone walls took on a raw, unequalled beauty. We banged and hollered on a door for what seemed like ages before a muttering old guardian shuffled along to swing open its heavy door. He led us through an inclined passage, roofed with beams and reeds, turned more massive wooden locks and waved us through.

We were confronted by open courtyards. One was long and narrow, another shaft-like with seven stories of cells. The honeycombed structure had almost 200 cubicles. All were secured with strong wooden doors, some with geometric symbols to ward off the evil eye.

As we explored, a man from a nearby village rode up on a mule to deposit his fat sack of provisions. He and the guardian sat silently, absorbed by the atmosphere. The sky darkened and a blustery wind howled through the *agadir*, pelting us with grit. Terrified kittens scrambled back to their guardian's dim room. I relished this perfect match of mood and place.

In the Ante-Atlas, these cells would be opened almost daily by the head of each family. Homes rarely kept more than a day's supply of food so that, as one 1930s French scholar was told, "women do not waste the good of God".

Earlier this century, Agadir Tasguent was known for its great age, storage capacity and the complexity of its constitution. The organisation and co-operation which sustained these granaries is palpable. For all the notorious chaos and anarchy of feudal Morocco, some were strictly, if not, equitably regulated. The starting point was the *louh*, a sort of written constitution or code which typically had between 200 and 300 articles setting out user's rights and duties. It covered everything from the use of weights and measures to repairing the roof and renting cells. Disobedience was dealt with by fines and sanctions.

There was a hierarchy, too, led by the oummal, trusted men of leading families who formed a Council of Notables or Governors. But their oligarchic rule could verge on tyrannical. Always above reproach, they often pocketed fines while their meetings were secret and inviolable. Merely to inspect the *louh* required payment and hospitality, a meal for example. Bottom of the rung were outsiders like travelling merchants whose tenure was distinctly precarious. It all sounded much like the governance of old Morocco itself — capricious and whimsical.

Tasguent remains in use today, but without the feudal necessity of the past. When the old guardian shuffles onto its roof, he no longer scans the hills and valleys for marauding tribesmen or thieves. There's no need of thorny hedges to line the ramparts or a lookout roster. Yet still he inhabits a room deep within its windowless walls, apparently reliant on water brought up by villagers. There's just one engaging concession to modern life; a doorbell.

In 1932 maverick artist and novelist Wyndham Lewis, published a Moroccan travelogue, 'Filibusters in Barbary'. With a French Protectorate official for company his travels included the *agadir* at Assads, one of the finest and best preserved examples in the Ante-Atlas. He made some earthy observations of some of the more bizarre misdemeanours and fines. Citing the 'Code of the Fortress of Beni Bahman' as typical he wrote:

"He who fornicates with a she-ass inside the agadir in view of the porter, or in view of any other witness (in whose testimony reliance may be placed) will pay a fine of 2 dirkem to the Oumanas [ie governors] and 3 sa'as of corn to the she-ass."

Lewis added dryly, that under Arab (presumably Makhzen) codes, such an offence would be punishable by death.

"What's a 'sa'as'?" I asked Hassan as we climbed the hill.

"What is that?" he replied.

I repeated my question several times, spitting and hacking it out in my most imaginative, mock Arabic tone. It never sounded right or familiar. All that came out was 'ass'. I tried to stifle a grin.

"*Ami*, what's so funny?"

Earlier Hassan had been sitting, still as a statue, in the shade of his home when our car crunched to a halt. Despite his heartfelt protests, we postponed the invitation home for tea, oranges, bread, and a friendly chat. After that I just didn't have the heart to share this bit of vulgarity and possibly offend him.

Hassan and I clattered over loose stones, occasionally snagging our sleeves on thorny argan trees, climbed and nibbled at by goats. Topping the ridge ahead, amidst those distinctive swirls of the Ante-Atlas was Assads' *agadir*.

Lewis' party had taken about an hour to reach the agadir, but that path straight up the sheer bluff was much too dangerous now. We improvised. As Hassan admitted he hadn't made this journey for years, a startled shepherd greeted us amidst tumbledown walls and weedy courtyards. The decades since Lewis' visit had clearly taken their toll. We sat gingerly on the roof and gazed back the way we'd come, beyond the mouth of the tranquil canyon and towards the hazy plains of the Souss.

The shepherd was intrigued by our visit. A German had rolled up a year or two earlier and walked in the hills, but no one had ever expressed the slightest bit of interest in feudal granaries. The village kids never ventured here any more because it was too dangerous, but like Hassan, they'd almost all come up at one time or another. This was *agadir* country; the shepherd pointed to others on loftier hills, all abandoned, forlorn and forgotten.

At his home we sat on stools in the courtyard, drinking mint tea and dipping warm flat bread in *amlou*, a delicious mix of argan oil, almond paste and honey. Hassan was on 'holiday', his quaint way of saying he was unemployed. Sure, there were computer jobs in Casablanca, but he preferred Agadir. It was closer, cheaper and nicer.

"We both like Agadir," he winked, "and you have found yours. Maybe I'll find mine, *inshallah*".

He could afford to be so choosy about a job. The family had a car which pounded the roads to Taroudannt, a larder full of food and treats, and teenage daughters who looked one in the eye without embarrassment or shame. It was time to continue my hunt for agadirs so we parted ways.

* * * * *

Days later I was hiking through a remoter part of the southern Ante-Atlas. Across the mountains beyond Tafraoute, the scenery is wilder and the people of more modest means. We emerged in Tizerkine Canyon to be dwarfed by ochre bluffs and cathedrals of rock. Brightly painted homes and the odd satellite dish distinguished new money from old hardship. We sat by the last house. Our hoped-for ride to town was unlikely since the regional weekly souk was days away and the only daily van had long gone.

An old man emerged, took one look at us and scuttled inside. Minutes later he appeared with a tray, cups, sugar and a tin of coffee.

"Sit down, *mes amis*, sit down here," he said as he tugged an extra stool from inside his yard. Bashir had driven trucks all over Europe and was now retired. Europe had been kind to him, and it seemed he wanted to give something back. I rather hoped there wouldn't be a lift for several days as he was a warm, engaging soul and they had a spare room. The hours passed as we talked of where we'd hiked and stayed.

"Do you know any *Chleuh* [Berber]?" he asked. I nodded at the gorge saying "Assif Tizerkine". He was delighted and we chatted earnestly about our treks. Bashir arched his eyebrows when, pointing vaguely at the hills, I said "*agadir*".

"*Agadir*? You know this thing?"

He chuckled, called his wife and they reminisced. There was the remote *agadir* in Kayko way up in the mountains, a place where a Spanish man kept horses. Then there was *agadir* in Ihrir Ououriz, about 12km up a side canyon, now abandoned but still in fine condition. They used to store things there themselves and his wife smiled at the memory. Soon after marrying in the 1950s they stopped renting their cell and life became considerably easier.

That night his wife prepared an enormous *tagine* and thick home-made bread. Before we ate, Bashir insisted on showing us his evening prayers. He spread his mat and acknowledged invisible *djinns* [spirits] by his shoulders, bad on the left, good on the right. "*C'est tout*," he announced after praying for a minute or two and leaving us to eat alone while he joined her in the kitchen.

They were good, kind people and I was sorry to leave. Bashir would have joined us. He loved the wild rugged beauty of these hills, but had recently fallen and his ankle wasn't up to it. We walked to the remote *agadir* of Ihrir Ououriz, another bit of nowhere in an unnamed canyon and I finally realised that part, or maybe most, of the appeal was the absolute stillness and haunting locations of these forgotten, lofty ruins.

They don't come much more still and haunting than here. Ihrir Ououriz was abandoned about 20 years ago because of a lack of water and its flat-roofed, stone houses lie empty and silent in the bend of an S-shaped canyon. An arched aqueduct crosses the bone-dry bed towards plots that perhaps always looked withered and scrawny and have now faded altogether.

Without knowing it's there, one might easily miss the agadir altogether. Its walls blend into the overhangs and recesses of a cliff and must have been extremely demanding to build. The door was padlocked, and for all I know, perhaps some eccentric still has things stashed away inside.

The *agadir* began perhaps 1000 years ago when the southern tribes were nomadic. From simple hiding places amidst rocks, developed chambers hollowed out of cliffs and caves. In turn came these distinctive granaries with villages huddled below. I don't lament their demise, for they are compelling reminders of a harsh life.

Survival required hoards, ramparts, lookouts and full cisterns — the last resort.

The Bedouin of the Negev

by Chris Doyle

I had been a vegetarian for almost ten years before that dinner. It had started early before the light disappeared but now I could no longer see what I was eating. Yesterday had been Eid al Adha, a Muslim holy day marking the end of the Ramadan fast, when traditionally a lamb is slaughtered and a feast is held. There was plenty left over but little else. Facing me, the recently diminished al-Batil flock was grazing twenty yards away. The brothers and sisters of what lay on my plate staring at my carnivorous nature. But it seemed too insensitive to embarrass my hosts by refusing the lamb they had cooked on a makeshift barbecue. I singed my fingers picking lamb dripping with fat off the hot grill.

"There are some Bedouin families who eat chicken on the Eid. They have no sheep left," Muhammad told me.

"So you eat beef," chimed in another of the brothers. "Ah, the British, they do not eat beef. *Majnuun* – crazy."

They laughed mockingly. One of them, Sulaiman, joked that mad cow disease was divine retribution for having left Palestine and given it all away to the Israelis.

Naively I whispered in Abd El Karims ear that I needed the toilet. "What!" he roared waving his arm, "everywhere here is a toilet!" Quite so

– no running water, no toilet. I made my way out to the edge of the plateau, their laughter followed me. The conversation continued late into the night underneath a lonely electric light bulb they rigged from their generator.

I had arrived at Beersheba bus station earlier that day. It was packed as I searched for my Bedouin host. If only he was wearing the traditional robes of the days of Lawrence and the Arab revolt, I might have spotted him. But this was modern Israel and he was a Bedouin in a modern state. Wearing neatly pressed black trousers and a white shirt, he outshone my bedraggled, crumpled look.

Abd El Karim Al Uttaiga was the Negev representative of the Association of Forty, a group set up in 1988 to fight for the rights of unofficial villages in Israel. The villages do not exist, says the Israeli government, and can be found on no official map. They are refused municipal services and survive with no mains electricity, water, sewage systems, schools, health or community centres. About half the Bedouin live in these villages.

We drove north out of the city past new, white, shimmering suburbs built for recent Jewish immigrants. The roads are flat and smooth, with well looked-after pavements, dotted with shrubs and trees. A large military camp hugs the road. The landscape is shaped by a series of light green, gentle rolling hills, some areas of England looked more like desert than this.

As we drove through the region, Abd El Karim pointed out various places that used to belong to one of the tribes.

"Most of them were expelled to Jordan," he said referring to the creation of Israel in 1948. The Palestinians call it 'al Nakba', the catastrophe. "After the war, the remaining Bedouin were rounded up into a reservation to the north and east of Beersheba, where most remain."

The town of Rahat was home to around 30,000 Bedouin.

"It is a township," explained Abd El Karim, "the Israeli government built it for us in 1971. They were trying to force the tribes away from their lands into seven towns like this one."

But Rahat was encircled by a series of shanty encampments and in one of these, Al-Batil, lived Abd El Karim and his family. We passed onto a dirt track, crossed a rickety bridge and headed across the fields to one particular collection of shacks situated on a plateau.

Abd El Karims barefoot children formed a welcoming committee greeting me with a shrill *Shalom*, in the belief that any white man must be Israeli. Despite appearing unconvinced that I was *ingleezi*, their smiles showed me they would make me welcome. The girls stood off at a distance giggling as a very formal ceremony began. The eldest son and I kicked a football to each other as the others watched on transfixed. Though I may not have overly impressed I was glad I could make friends with the children, they make up half the Bedouin.

A series of tents and shacks constituted the encampment, some covered with black plastic netting rather than traditional woven goats hair. Others were mere heaps of rusted corrugated iron. One or two of the buildings had concrete walls but neatly hidden beneath the outer tent. Apparently, they did not want the police to know that there was a permanent structure underneath for fear that it would be demolished. Rubbish lay strewn everywhere on the dry ground cascading down the sides of the hill and there was even the shell of a burnt out car.

My room was not unusual in its cell-like construction: neither windows nor light bulbs interrupted the plainness of the walls. But walking around the camp I was imbued with a profound sense of the pride of its inhabitants, trying to make the best of a tough deal.

Having taken on the kids it was now time for the men who had gathered to greet me in the formal room or *shiqqa*. The men sitting in the *shiqqa* were nearly all Abd El Karims brothers. With a birth rate of well over five per cent, Bedouin families with ten children are not uncommon. The Bedouin reputation for hospitality was not a myth. Existing on an ultra-high dosage of caffeine they made life for an insomniac like me very difficult. But the coffee was thick and bitter and the tea perfumed with mariamiya, a variety of wild sage making refusal impossible. As the conversation continued it was disturbed only by the regular gentle ringing of mobile phones. With no access to land lines the mobile has become a standard accoutrement of a young Bedouins life.

"Most of us do not work on the land anymore," said Abd el Karim. "We have a small flock of sheep and goats. But we have no land left."

"What do you want?"

"Just to be farmers. Thats what we are. We are citizens of Israel and we are happy with that but this is not fair. They can make all the Arabs into Israeli friends but instead they make enemies of us."

This was a refrain I was to become used to: emphasis on their Israeli citizenship as they felt vulnerable and insecure, scared to acknowledge their Palestinian roots or Bedouin heritage. But despite their desire to be farmers, the majority of the Negev Bedouin gave up a nomadic existence for a pastoral way of life even before the creation of Israel.

Rahat appeared like so many places I had seen in the Middle East, a festering, unfinished construction site. The birth rate is so high that when one floor is finished a new one is soon needed. Whilst Rahat had the basic infrastructure that Al Batil and the unrecognised villages lacked, there was still no sewage network and around half were unemployed. Abd El Karim complained that Rahat was little more than a Bedouin dormitory estate for Beersheba.

"We are just cheap labour. There is no industry here. No jobs. Everyone who can, works in Beersheba in building or transport".

A depressing, sterile atmosphere hung over Rahat, as I noticed that it was nearly all houses and nothing else with only a handful of shops and restaurants.

"Even for those who do go to school the drop-out rate is massive. Few graduate," said Jason Greenberg a teacher at the local school. "The facilities are pitiful there aren't enough desks or teaching materials."

But that was not the only problem with the town. "There are bad relations between people," a Bedouin from the Al Huzeiyal tribe told me about the problems of Rahat. "They are not ready to be in the city and there is much feuding and drugs. We are not used to living right on top of each other. Bedouin are used to space and privacy. It does not suit our rhythm of life. But we have no choice."

Abd El Karim took me to another resettlement township, Lakkiya. Smaller than Rahat and less crowded, at first it appeared more appealing but it suffered from similar problems. Squeezed between the buildings were the black tents of Bedouin, whilst again unrecognised encampments lay scattered around the periphery. On the hill, Abd El Karim showed me the remains of a demolished house. A tree grew in the middle of where it had stood. A young boy showed us two more demolished buildings close by. They had been deemed illegal as they fell outside the zone for residential building. The court had given the owner around six months to demolish his own house. Endangered buildings in the Negev number in the thousands.

Al Batil had not been under immediate threat from the authorities. But over a thousand members of the Tarabin-a-Sane, who have suffered being uprooted twice in recent history, faced forcible eviction to make way for the expansion of a Beersheba suburb. They assured me that this time they would not move. I looked out over a 100-metre stretch of bare ground that led up to the sparkling well-watered neighbourhood of Omer, with the second highest *per capita* income in Israel. The area closest to the Bedouin was under construction and separated by a high fence. This part had yet to be greened – no trees but the shells of the houses were all there. Many of the Tarabin had helped to build them, but they were not welcomed as residents.

The older section of Omer was more akin to the southern Mediterranean with lush villas, swimming pools and BMW convertibles. One resident told me that life was pleasant there, quiet with few worries. "The Bedouin can just be moved. They can live anywhere. They always have done."

Driving further away from Beersheba, there was the beginning of a new shanty zone.

"What's that village?"

"Abu Kaff."

"Can we go there?"

Abd El Karim looked a little uncertain but we came off the road. Out came the mobile and the requisite permission was sought. Bedouin in the Negev are suspicious of strangers because of informants who check to ensure that they have built no permanent structures. Then came Abd El Karims puncture. Commonplace for the residents of the illegal villages because of the awful state of the tracks but with few resources and little money available a relatively minor problem like a burst tyre could keep a car off the road for a while. The inner tyre was laced with the patch marks of previous punctures.

We approached one area of the encampment to the right. We were ushered into a concrete-floored *shiqqa*. Within minutes, we had attracted quite a gathering. Abd El Karim slipped into politics, explaining the benefits of his party, Tajammua. On the wall behind me was an election poster for the current Israeli Prime Minister, Bibi Netanyahu, as bold and smiling as ever. No graffiti, no offensive language. It appeared that this was not a joke. Some of the Bedouin do vote Likud. In Rahat, I had seen a

Netanyahu election caravan. I inquired after the poster and got a peremptory shrug as if to say "they are all the same."

Ali offered me a tour, a hastily accepted offer, as I viewed with disquiet a fourth cup of coffee arriving. He had difficulty speaking in Arabic without slipping into Hebrew and his wife acted as interpreter. According to Ali, there were some 400 families here. They showed me the inside of their home. Again there were no electric lights and no windows.

"We get some water but only in the house." There was a miserable trickle eking out of the tap. The issue of water clearly rankled with Ali. "Look at this land. No water! No water! All the olive trees are dead. Look over there!" In the distance, we could make out some dark green acreage. "Jewish land. They have all the water they want. They eat our land and drink our water." He pointed to the nearby electricity pylons. Even though they were so close, the Bedouin could not tap into the mains electricity.

Round the back of the house, a dried up river-bed separated the community from the next field. "In the winter the children have to walk through the river. They then go four kilometres by foot to school."

So far my journey had revolved around reservation areas, but I wanted to venture further south of Beersheba into the heart of the Negev. Many Bedouin still lived outside the reservation where they are no longer allowed to graze their herds. Here the Negev starts to look the part; the terrain is drier, craggier, with vast *wadis* and canyons. A stray camel even dared to charge the car.

Cedric Parizot was a French anthropologist studying at Ben Gurion University south of Beersheba. He agreed to take me to see an old friend of his from the Azazmeh tribe. We headed down yet another dirt track. It was in an appreciably better state than the ones around Rahat. "That's because the military made this," he explained.

On both sides of the track, there was evidence of vain attempts to cultivate the land. There was such little water that a state of emergency was expected to be declared before the end of the year. Nothing would be growing in this *wadi*.

I could now make out the black specks of a couple of Bedouin shanties. Unlike at Al-Batil these were not clustered together but spread right out across the valley, perhaps twenty in all. What would it be like during the winter when it reached five degrees below freezing?

Salman Abu Auda Abu Jalidan was an old man with traditional headdress but wearing a bright orange shirt. He had blackened teeth, and a watch that dangled from his wrist. Salman was thin and gaunt, but carried an air of dignity. Even he had progressed to having a mobile. He ushered us into his *shiqqa* greeting Cedric with the Arabic, Idriss, that the Bedouin had given him in honour of their close friendship.

The youngest of Salmans ten children were called Yasser and Suha, after the President and First Lady of Palestine. Arabs have a habit of naming children after personalities: in 1993, a number of Palestinian families in Gaza had named their children 'FAFO' after the Norwegian institute which had hosted the Oslo peace talks.

Salmans story was one of loss of land, his flock and most of his tribe. In passionate terms, he described the whole series of court cases dating back to 1979 aiming to deprive him of his land. He had no flocks left, no means of income. In 1981 alone, he said, they took 230 of his goats. They were the Green Patrol, a paramilitary unit set up by Ariel Sharon when Minister of Agriculture essentially to control the Bedouin. The patrol has slaughtered hundreds of thousands of animals belonging to Bedouin in its twenty-two year history. Even then, Salman had very little area in which to graze his livestock. He was surrounded by military areas but none of this was marked out.

Military zones take up much of the Negev not devoted to nature reserves. Every few kilometres on the main road, there had been signs alerting you to firing ranges on the sides of the road. Signs for readers of Hebrew and English, that is. A few Hebrew signs had had a tiny part in Arabic recently stuck on to the board. But this was so small as to be almost illegible from a car.

"They even took my tractor because they claimed that I was stealing water."

"How come?"

"I had to take it from a tank so I used my tractor. They confiscated it."

"You have no water here?"

"I do now. After they killed my nephew last year they allowed us to have water but not for agriculture."

"They killed your nephew?"

"Yes"

His nephew had been shot in somewhat bizarre circumstances. The sequence of events was unclear. But Salman was enraged that the Israeli authorities had refused to set up an inquiry into what had happened. He felt that the man responsible would never be apprehended.

Cedric explained that Salman "cannot build anything that resembles a permanent structure here or it is liable to be demolished. They destroyed a dam he built. The Green Patrol takes aerial pictures to check that there are no violations." Salman protested that he cannot even plant any trees.

His small rusting generator was forty paces from his shack. It had no protection from the elements and could provide only minimal power. He turned it on for a few hours every evening. Around his shack was a wealth of rusting cans and plastic. He and his family were totally reliant on what the state offered. At Al-Batil, the Uttaiga family could take advantage of what little Rahat had to offer. But this *wadi* was so barren and isolated that it was hard to imagine how Salman survived.

A short way down the *wadi* lived Salmans brother whose son had been killed. Like Salman, he was chronically in debt. His son had been the bread-winner of the family.

"If only Kofi Annan would come by himself he would then know," he fumed. "The English and the Turks never did this, took the land of the Bedouin. Its the fault of the Americans for helping the Jews."

We returned to the peaceful leafy Kibbutz at Sede Boker. Ben Gurion, Israels founder and first Prime Minister, is buried here and little black pipes run from shrub to tree irrigating them efficiently, all working to carry out the great leaders vision of greening the Negev. Nearby are the silvery panels of a solar energy information centre. The shelves of the supermarket are crammed with a host of fruit and vegetables. I shopped alongside two Israelis in T-shirts. Here it seemed so natural for them to have machine guns slung over their shoulders. I wondered how they felt. Here in this enclosed little oasis the desert was blooming and life was beautiful.

Tal was a ranger for the Israeli Nature Reserves Authority (NRA). Many of the Bedouin had cited the NRA as being hostile to them. Since the NRA controlled around two thirds of the Negev this clash was not surprising. The Authority accuses the Bedouin of overgrazing increasing the likelihood of desertification. The Bedouin claim that they have no choice, given the diminishing area that they can use.

For Tal, the Bedouin can be a problem. "They steal. They are really exceptional at it. They can ghost up behind you and without realising it your radio has gone. They will steal anything. There was a case this week. A buggy was taken. We know it's them."

"Why do they do it?"

"Well, they know the area backwards."

Tal explained to me the role of the NRA. It was set up to look after the environment all over Israel.

"Who does the hunting?"

"The Druze are really keen. They come all the way down from the north. They leave in the middle of the night just to get down here. "

In the Negev there are still populations of leopard and wolves, foxes, ibex and gazelle but these species are endangered and are all protected from the hunters.

Sede Boker overlooked a canyon where numerous hikers made camp fires. It was Pessach, the Jewish Passover, and the Negev was packed with eager trekkers and campers with four wheeled jeeps.

Tal pointed out that the wood for the fires had to be brought in from outside the nature reserve in order not to disturb the delicate ecosystem.

"One of the Azazmeh," says Cedric "told me that a member of the Green Patrol came out to his camp in the night and they had coffee by the fire. The officer then asked the Bedouin where the wood came from. Naturally, the Bedouin pointed to an area close by. This resulted in an on-the-spot fine."

Tal retorted: "You cannot believe everything they say. Really before the NRA was founded in 1964 people just shot anything in the Negev. You see there was nobody living here in the Negev then."

"Oh! Weren't the Bedouin here then?" I asked.

"No, they all came from the Sinai after that."

This was not the moment to start debating British Mandate figures which showed that in 1932 there were nearly 50,000 Negev Bedouin. Tal believed that a people without a land took a land without a people, the desert was therefore empty and later the NRA was ready to step in and stop the newcomers from ruining it.

He was by no means all hostile to the Bedouin. He worked with Id, a Bedouin ranger who lived in a Bedouin shanty at Ramat Hovav, a dozen kilometres south of Beersheba. I had visited there earlier that day. On one side of the road was Israel's only toxic waste treatment plant. On the other were the shacks of hundreds of Bedouin. The air had been laden with the foul stench of chemicals. Newspaper reports indicated that it might soon be closed for environmental reasons. Tal sympathised with their plight. "Yes the situation there is quite terrible. They all have lung and eye problems."

I looked out over the Makhtesh Ramon, Israel's 'Grand Canyon'. At one point Bedouin would have camped there in this a desert that they had lived on for centuries. Only 13,000 Bedouin remained in the Negev after 1951 out of a 1948 population of 65–95,000. That number is falling still as the people abandon their traditional ways, and move to the stifling environment of the resettlement towns. Tourists now swarmed around the shop buying Bedouin trinkets, clothes and coffee pots. This was the image that they take back home, preserving the Bedouin souvenirs in their minds and on their mantelpieces but leaving the future for the Bedouin uncertain.

A Saudi Journey

by Ed Waller

Gripping the corners of his headscarf between *nargila*-stained teeth so his face was totally hidden, he looked like a Bedouin legionnaire. His gnarled fists seemed as though they'd once brandished an old Winchester rifle as he galloped on a camel with Lawrence of Arabia against the Turks.

Instead he was a truck driver, taking me and a dirty old fuel tanker south through Saudi Arabia's Hejaz mountains. And those fists were quite happy doing 360 degree spins on the steering wheel, as we careered around hairpin turns. His name was Ammar and the only English he spoke was 'seat belt'. I was already wearing it.

To take my mind off his creative driving I peered through the brown windscreen. An endless litter of flattened signs, exploded tyres, rusting vehicle wrecks and camel carcasses lined the roadside. It didn't exactly inspire confidence in Saudi road safety. We'd already had to slalom around a few camels as they ambled across the highway or, worse, sat stubbornly on the warm tarmac. Still, I thought, only 13 hours to go.

Two evenings ago I'd been relaxing on a beach by the Red Sea. The tide was more oily black than red, bobbing with old Mirinda cans and less pleasant flotsam. Still, it was the last stretch of open water I'd see for a long time. Nearby was the ancient city of Mecca, the spiritual heart of Islam and destination for millions of *Hajj* pilgrims every year. However my destination was not this ancient site, but the brand new port of Dubai, the throbbing commercial centre of the oil-drenched Gulf. In the intervening 1000 miles of desert I hoped to meet some of the Arabs that didn't fit the conventional stereotypes of zealot and oil-sheikh. My first stop lay sprawling before me — the shimmering new offices and ramshackle old town of Saudi's second biggest city, Jeddah.

Many cities claim they never sleep; Jeddah is not one of them. It snores, it yawns and by about 11pm all I had for company were scavenging cats. Even the police stopped me in the street and told me to go to bed. They had guns. I went to bed.

By day the new city's topiary-lined boulevards were jammed with gleaming Toyotas and old Chevrolets, while the narrow capillaries of the old city were clogged with trolley-pushers, ferrying wares around the stalls. Purdah-clad old women presided over little piles of waxy natural chewing gum or bundles of miswak, the short sticks Saudis use to clean their teeth. Old men sat with bathroom scales or typewriters, forlornly offering their services.

Rubble was piled by the roadside. Sometimes it was coral bricks dragged up from the ocean, other piles came from tumble-down colonial buildings, their once elegant wooden balconies now lop-sided.

You can measure devotion to Islam, state-enforced or otherwise, from the little things: shop signs saying 'closed for prayer'; arrows in hotel rooms showing Mecca's direction; the 500-strong praying crowds that often blocked side-streets or the *Matawwa*, the religious police, punishing somebody for washing his car during prayer time.

Apart from a few shops around the Corniche, Jeddah's hard-working *souks* are pretty much devoid of the cheap trinkets Westerners associate with Arabia. Instead they're filled with far more useful things like sewing machines, textiles and engine parts. This is not the land that tourism forgot, but the one whose government actively discourages the influx of snap-happy, under-dressed visitors that other countries rely on. And since there's no such thing as a tourist visa, it's assumed you're there to work — after all, everyone else is.

Only about half the kingdom's 16 million inhabitants are Saudi; the rest are an industrial army of Asians, Africans and Turks who inhabit the lower slopes of the social pyramid. Although many of Jeddah's visiting pilgrims stay and work, with or without a permit, they stoically accept that, as non-nationals, they are second-class citizens.

Though the gulf between most Saudis and the guest workers ensures the kingdom is no cultural mixing-pot, its reliance on immigrants is reflected in its street food. Sugary wafts from Bengali sweets compete for nostril space with curries, chow-meins, barbecues and kebabs. Sizzling away on four-foot steel frying-platters are various viscera , chopped up with yoghurt and spices by Punjabi stallholders wielding paint-scrapers like daggers. Stalls sold Filipino kebabs garnished with anything from sweet 'n' sour sauce to Swiss cheese and, in what I took to be a potent symbol of East meets West, they are served Breville-toasted in hot dog rolls.

Uniting these various nationalities is tea. Ultra-sweet mint tea, without milk — anything else is not an option. The pavements are peppered with innumerable soggy offerings bearing Lipton's yellow label. Saudi nightlife revolves around tea and the open air teahouse where men, and only men, gather after the working day is done. Close your eyes and the noise alone lets you know you are a long way from home: the clatter of the backgammon chips slapped down with manly gusto; the bubbling of nargila pipes laden with sweet tobacco; the endless shuffling of slip-on shoes; and, of course, the mournful *muezzin* calling the faithful to prayer. "In Saudi, there's too much praying," grumbled Zubair, an old Indian, through his smoke-yellowed beard, "and not enough women," he added with a wink.

The nearest this non-Muslim got to Mecca was a dusty intersection, a few miles outside the city of El-Taif. Ammar's old tanker eventually appeared through the heat-haze and soon I was in the mountains. The Hejaz range stretches down Saudi's west coast, rising slowly to Jebel Sawdah, some 2900 metres above the Red Sea.

The road wound through a gravel wasteland, dotted with startled-looking trees that were like umbrellas blown inside out. It got quite cold on those slopes, and we often drove through thick, wet clouds. Throughout the long drive we stopped at several teahouses and shared pipes with fellow drivers, usually immigrants. After a few glasses, and maybe a quick prayer, Ammar would jangle his keys and we'd be off again.

From this cross-section of guest workers, I got the distinct message that the Saudi regime was something they tolerated so they could make money for their families at home. "If you can live in Saudi," said a Kenyan bus driver, "you can live anywhere on earth." Being a Christian, he found

Saudi's religious laws hardest to take. He spoke furtively of secret meetings with Filipinos where, for a couple of stolen hours, they'd worship their illegal God together. Not many had good words for their hosts, particularly the *Matawwa*, calling them 'double-zeros', after the two loops of black rope they hung around their head scarves. Women were 'ninjas', after their all-black, head-to-toe *chadors*, through which only their eyes could be seen.

Ammar eventually handed me over to a couple of Saudis who were driving further south, and I was squeezed into the back of a tiny Suzuki pick-up with three enormous Filipino labourers who used my backpack as a cushion. The driver wanted to take me to his friend's hotel in somewhere called Khemis Mushayt. It was 3am and I was lost in the mountains with only 60 riyals and four small bananas to my name. I was in no position to refuse.

Khemis Mushayt will never feature on any 'must-see' tourist itinerary and the city has little to offer in the way of Kodak moments. But an evening spent wandering the narrow streets provided a glimpse of Saudi realism.

Industrious smiths and tailors peered out from unfinished and unpicturesque concrete buildings. The streets were full of watch repairers and empty international freight agencies. But after last prayer the town seemed to change personality. Its *souks* came alive with young locals indulging in Saudi's favourite evening pursuit — walking up and down the main drag.

It was time to move on and I shared a taxi with six others to my next stop, Najran, down on the baking desert flats. As we drove the cloud-clad mountains were replaced by teetering piles of smooth boulders, which were in turn replaced by crumbling ancient *mesas*. We were occasionally besieged by marauding gangs of baboons, 100 at a time, but after a while even they left us alone. Apart from the frequent police check-points and the odd patch of greenery that some poor soul had the job of cultivating, we could have been on Mars's boulder-strewn orange surface.

It was getting hot. Sweat condensed on the windows, and opening them was like opening the door of a blast furnace. Things got worse after we picked up a couple of old men with orange beards and I had to go in the back with the luggage. The sun seemed to swell even larger in the cloudless sky and I began to think of that murky Red Sea beach back in Jeddah. At some dismal junction a mesh-sided truck stuffed with goats pulled up beside us and one of the poor creatures and I exchanged a poignant glance. It was truly a moment of shared understanding.

Outside Najran I made my first mistake. We'd stopped for tea and shade near the border and I was photographing the desertscape. Within seconds angry police arrived and confiscated my camera. It got worse when they found my zoom lens, and even more so when they discovered the mini-disc recorder and microphone. Since tourism didn't exist, I was obviously a spy, sent to photograph their border security. To really make their day, I didn't have my passport with me.

After much shouting and exposing of film on their part, and apologising and exposing of paperwork on mine, a passing Filipino explained the concept of tourism. The police eventually returned my equipment and sent me away with a simple warning: do not photograph anything.

So when Abbas pulled up in an Oldsmobile and offered me a guided tour of 'his town'. I gratefully accepted. Though kitted out in the full Saudi uniform, white *dishdasha* and red head scarf, what came out of Abbas's mouth was a mixture of gangsta rap lyric and Californian valley-speak cliché. Saudi women were either 'bitches' or 'babes', the *Matawwa* were 'assholes' and Najran was 'bum nowhere'.

Abbas was rich. His father was somebody in the Government and he'd been educated in London and the US. From his air-conditioned saloon we explored the many examples of old Arabic mud-and-straw architecture that Najran hides behind its low-rise breeze-blocks. Safely hiding behind the high walls of his brother-in-law's house, Abbas conjured up a few bottles of beer — real, cold beer — and together we watched his favourite Arnold Schwartzeneggar film, wallowing in sin and crime.

There was enough mud-and-straw, and beer, to keep us busy for a few days before another shared taxi took me to Sharurah, deep in the Empty Quarter — a fairly accurate description for an area the size of Germany that contains nothing but sand. No trees, no rocks, just sand. Curving dunes towered 30 feet over us, capped with the exposed corners of abandoned vehicles, long since reclaimed by the desert. The shifting sands had even tried to take back our thin strip of tarmac, and we had to drive carefully over dunes until we found it again. The only other car we passed on that three-hour trip was parked, it's driver praying by the roadside.

I arrived in Sharurah just as the *Matawwa's* weekly public beating was drawing to a close. Fakim, the Syrian who'd been feeding me Glacier Mints throughout the taxi trip through the Empty Quarter, said they were punishing a "thiefman-dangerman". I spent the evening in his home, a one-room breeze-block cube that was about 15 feet square and furnished with a bed, a table and a bookshelf. The mints were replaced by a plate of raw carrots and some fruit, and we discussed the relative merits of Shakespeare, Gorky and Moliere, about whom he knew a lot more than I. He also told me about his family in Syria and his house and boat back in Latakia. He seemed to be counting the days until he returned.

Apologising for the rubble in one corner, he explained that a neighbour had been busted for drugs, so Fakim simply walled up his original front door and knocked through a new one overlooking another, more respectable, road.

The next morning I made my second mistake — trying to hitch across the rest of the Empty Quarter. This time the police were more bemused than angry. They eventually let me go, even dropping me off at the bus station. Saudi buses are actually quite pleasant, punctual and, since travel is strictly controlled by the Government, quite empty. I was the only passenger and Ahmed, my Turkish driver, made me sit next to him so he could regale me with manly tales of Istanbul nights as we crossed the desert to Riyadh.

The hot, dusty and dry Saudi capital squats amid featureless desert flats. Few buildings are more than 50 years old, and most are not even half that. The name Riyadh comes from the Arabic word for garden, as the occasional pansy-filled roundabout testifies. Tall gates and armed guards separate the diplomatic quarter where sweaty Western businessmen enjoy *apres*-conference boozing in embassy parties from the rest of the city. But for most of Riyadh's population, the days are an endless cycle of "too much hot, too much work, too much cold," as Ahmed had warned me.

Judging by the number of kids wearing tattered versions of the national strip, football is one of the few areas where Saudis can channel their passions given the prohibition on cinemas, theatres and almost every form of public entertainment. Many Saudis told me they'd been "sad for a month" following a recent defeat at the hands of England. A result, that much to the chagrin of the queue behind me, Mohamed the bank teller and I spent a good 20 minutes discussing as we debated whether the Al-Nasr striker Majid Abdullah was in the same league as Manchester United's David Beckham. He professed to be United's biggest fan, even risking a healthy fine to watch matches live on the prohibited satellite TV.

That evening Mohamed drove me to the King Fahd stadium to watch the local team, Al-Hilal, play Al-Ahli from Jeddah. Saudi youth was out in force. The snack of choice was dried seeds and their husks filled the aisles, crunching underfoot with every step. This was the only place in the kingdom where I'd seen Saudis outnumber immigrants. The only non-nationals were Pakistanis who weaved between the rows, selling neatly-wrapped slices of cake.

Like every away crowd, the visitors were the more vocal, drumming and chanting, and wearing *dishdashas* in their team's colours of green and white. Others had colour co-ordinated head scarves and even cheerleader pom-poms. Hilal's firm sat silently in rows, a uniform sea of white and red head scarves, chomping sullenly on their seeds and spitting them pointedly.

As Al-Ahli's domination of the game grew, their fans became more rowdy. The riot-police, who'd spent the first half simply watching the match, began to close in. They were greeted with increased chanting, lobbed Pepsi cartons and the occasional fireworks. Even the military band which marched around at half-time faced loud jeers and missiles. Compared with their firm grip over other aspects of Saudi life, the police were surprisingly tolerant — perhaps because the fans were all nationals. Al-Ahli won, and Mohamed and I spent the journey home deep in therapeutic post-mortem. He was a Hilal fan.

One afternoon in Riyadh I journeyed out to the Janariah camel market — the largest in the Middle East. I don't know the collective noun for camels, but after spending many hours in their company, I would suggest it should be an 'ugliness', or perhaps a 'stubbornness'. Either way, one is permanently gathered on the outskirts of the capital. There I met Majid, and we had tea with the Bedouin herders. They stood in stiff upright poses for my camera, though joked around when it was safely packed away. One even pretended to call the *Matawwa* after a male camel ended up in the same truck as a female one.

Lorries and pick-up trucks began to arrive from the surrounding Bedouin stables, laden with what Majid called 'the shits of the desert'. The camels sat contentedly in the back of the trucks. When standing they seemed equally untroubled by what was going on around them. The problem lay in getting them from one position to the other. Spitting and roaring, they loudly let it be known that they were not happy camels. Mass shoulder charges proved most effective, but the more resourceful used industrial cranes.

Once the Bedouins sprayed the buyer's name in red paint on the camel's flank, the animals knew their next stop was the abattoir. That's when they became really stroppy and slipped their rope hobble or made a three-legged stumble to the surrounding stables. The young camel herders would charge off with ropes, trying to lasso the errant beast while avoiding its vicious kicks. Camel-wrestling doesn't look that much fun, but it's a great spectator sport.

Majid was there to monitor inflation in camel prices, rising due to the forthcoming Eid feast when camel meat is traditionally eaten. Having chewed through a tough joint of boiled camel meat during the ride from the Empty Quarter, I could only sympathise. "But you eat pigs," said Majid, misinterpreting my raised eyebrow.

Not being married, Majid was allowed to invite his five cousins and I back to his place for the evening. He had a large modern house, fitted with plush wall-to-wall carpets. But in the main lounge, aside from a few cuboid cushions, the only items were a new widescreen TV and, in pride of place, a Sony PlayStation.

FIFA '98 was the name of the game, and all those years of having nothing else to do in the evenings had made my hosts experts. My thumb-action, however, needed some work. Majid was always England so I was Saudi. It was a walk-over — Alan Shearer scored a hat-trick in the last 15 minutes and my ears, as they had the previous night, rang with the Arabic equivalent of 'here we go, here we go, here we go'.

Mid-way through the four-hour marathon, I noticed the Indian. He supplied tea and cardamom coffee, mopped up spillages, never saying more than a few necessary words. I'd initially assumed he was another of Majid's mates, but it soon dawned on me that he was his servant. During a rematch of the 1966 World Cup final between England and Germany I asked Majid why he needed a servant. "I told you," he said, as he scored again. "I'm not married."

The next morning Majid drove me to the train station and we stopped at 'Chop-Chop' Square near Riyadh's central mosque. He explained to me the Saudi theory of deterrence and family vengeance rather than rehabilitation, and how the *Matawwa* carefully lay down piles of sand to soak up the executee's blood. "It doesn't happen very often," he assured me, without sarcasm. "Maybe once a month."

Since the British bombed the Ottoman-built Hejaz Railway during the First World War, the track between Riyadh and Dammam is the only working rail link in Saudi. Next morning, thumbs still aching from the PlayStation marathon, I was aboard, sampling its atrocious egg rolls. Since there's not much to avoid in the Eastern Province, the route is pretty straight, and soon we were amid the verdant forest of telecommunications towers, electricity pylons and factory chimneys that grow around the capital. Because the track is only used six times a day, the camels claim it as their own even more than they do the roads. They stand chewing nonchalantly only metres from passing locomotives, mouthing "we were here first".

The journey was filled by exchanging banter with Saudi students and rig-workers on their way back to the Gulf. They managed to combine boasts about their sexual conquests with curiosity about western women. Their fascination with women and beer seemed proportional to how much the Government tried to control them. We were interrupted by the train stopping abruptly in the middle of the desert. The carriages shunted back and forth for a few minutes as railway officials rushed about, until we slowly pulled away. The inquisitive, myself among them, leant from the open doors trying to see what had caused the hold up.

A camel had been cut almost exactly in half — not bad for the 30 miles-an-hour we were doing — and by the time we in the males-only, second-class carriage encountered it, the carcass had already attracted a shimmering film of bluebottles.

I arrived at the vast Al-Haas oasis with a profusion of date palms on either side. Among the irrigation channels a boy who'd been showing off on a rusty BMW showed me how easy it was to climb palm trees. From the tops I could see minarets and pylons poking up through the leaves. I discovered the city of Whiff nestled deep within the trees, its perfumed *souks* offering everything from bottles of frankincense and sandalwood to cheap Western toilet water. The surrounding oasis extended for miles; the stuff of Arabian Nights, full, as the advertisement says, of eastern promise. But my visa was about to expire.

Saudi bureaucracy reached its zenith as I crossed the United Arab Emirates border. After long queues, bus tickets in triplicate, much rubber-stamping and a 12-hour drive, I awoke to the sight of wooden dhows sailing down Dubai creek.

In the five-minute walk between Dubai's central bus-stop and the nearest no-star hotel, I was offered opium, hashish, heroin and my choice from Indian, Chinese, Russian or Kenyan women. "Very good sex," explained a helpful Indian, "only 200 dirhams." Something called "three-quarter sex" was a mere 100. Women drove cars and had their faces, and even hair, on public display — and there wasn't a Matawwa in sight. Solar-powered parking meters sprang up on the pavements, pagers and Walkmans appeared on people's belts, and signs on mosque doors had mobile phones crossed out with red lines. Things beeped on the hour, and video billboards topped space-age towers inviting people to do business on the Internet.

As much as I'd like to describe Dubai as the westernised, technology-obsessed Hong Kong of the Middle East, as the in-flight magazines do, it isn't. Of course the West has left its marks — baseball caps instead of head-dresses — but it will take more than a few decades of oil and tourism to change 1400 years of Islam. Buses are still segregated; Fridays bring pavements clogged with South Asians at prayer, and mountains of slip-on shoes accumulate outside mosques, just as they do in Saudi. And though the north side of Dubai creek is dwarfed by futuristic architecture, one of the biggest and newest constructions on the south side is a shiny new mosque.

Dubai is certainly cosmopolitan but South Asia's influences are far more apparent than the West's. The latter is restricted to only a few places; five-star hotels where even the toilet-hoses supply warm water; boozy bars, where US sailors chat up women from Sheffield; or private beaches where ex-pats' daughters strut around in bikinis, eagerly eyed by clusters of locals and the occasional travel writer.

I sat looking out across the Arabian Gulf and took off my boots. Inside was sand from the Empty Quarter, which I slowly poured on to its long lost kin on the beach. The pure orange grains sat uncomfortably on top of the local white sand, peppered with fag ends and the little plastic bits from water bottle tops. For a few moments it stood out as a little patch of unsullied desert, proud like the Bedouin at Janariah. But before my feet had even touched the warm ocean, the incoming tide had turned it into just another bit of beach.

On the Banks of the Euphrates

by Penny Young

I leant my bicycle against the railings of the French suspension bridge and gazed down at the oily waters gulping and swirling murkily below. As I stared in awe at the Euphrates River, the people of Deir Ez Zor, who had come to admire the sunset and sip sweet tea in the riverside cafes, stared at me in equal amazement. The dusty little town in the eastern Syrian desert, more than 300 miles East of Damascus, perched on the banks of one of history's mightiest rivers, doesn't see too many tourists. Sporadic wars and unrest in the Middle East, coupled with an uneasy relationship with the West, keep many would-be visitors away. The US persists in including Syria on a list of what it terms 'terrorist countries', which makes the Syrians laugh hollowly, especially when American and British bombs are dropped on Iraq next door.

I'd arrived in Deir Ez Zor by a circuitous route which had begun a week or so earlier when I flew into the capital, Damascus. You can smell the politics as soon as you get off the plane and walk into the arrivals lounge, lavishly decorated with pictures of the Syrian President, Hafiz Assad who took power in 1970 after a series of coups and power struggles which followed the French withdrawal in 1946. During my trip, he was about to be 'elected' (there were no other candidates) by a 99.98 per cent majority for his fifth seven-year term.

As I cycled down the long straight road from the airport into Damascus, I admired several huge portraits of the President and his two sons, Bashar and Basel, who died in a car accident five years ago. I was particularly impressed by the ones in which they all wear impenetrable sunglasses. In Damascus, the Al Haramein Hotel was full to capacity so they gave me a couch in the hotel office. An oversized photograph of Mr Assad looked down at me from one of the walls. I felt as if I were sleeping with the President.

I was here to follow the Euphrates River through Syria. One of the great rivers of the Middle East, the Euphrates cuts its way from the Black Sea mountains of Turkey through Anatolia, into the eastern Syrian deserts and down into Iraq where it meets the Tigris and spills out into the Persian Gulf. It has been the lifeblood of many civilisations who built their green and pleasant cities along its fertile banks. The Mesopotamians, Babylonians, Seleucids, Romans, Byzantines, Persians, Omayyads and Abbasids — they all had their moments of glory and left their mark.

My first sighting of the river came from the window of a mini-bus on the road from Aleppo to Raqqa. A blue sliver of water appeared, snaking its way through the flat mud-brown desert. The startling thing about the Euphrates is that it is there at all. In Egypt, the land on either side of the River Nile is heavily cultivated. In Syria, the Euphrates seems to move through a never ending landscape of emptiness, apart from the odd cultivated patch of sublime, emerald green. People toil on the land, their heads swathed in head scarves and veils to protect themselves from the wind and flies. Bent double, they dig where their ancestors and invaders dug thousands of years ago. Flocks of sheep, watched over by shepherd boys and girls on donkeys, wander endlessly over the dusty plains. I wondered what they would eat when they've eaten everything?

The next day I caught the bus from Raqqa to the town of Althawra. I wanted to cycle out to Lake Assad and its dam on the Euphrates. My bicycle was strapped on top of the bus, but as we drove along there was an anxious tapping above my head. One of the wheels was bouncing on the roof.

"How much did your bike cost?" asked a passenger.

"Dollars," I said weakly. Somebody spoke to the driver and he pulled over at once, jumped out and tied the errant wheel down more firmly.

It was an eventful journey. A car had hurtled off the road moments before and was balanced precariously, swaying over a water trough. There was much tutting and head shaking inside the bus. At Mansura we stopped to pick up more passengers. A young couple asked how much it costs to go on to Aleppo.

"Seventy five Syrian pounds," said the driver. (About £1).

"It's 60 Syrian pounds," replied the couple indignantly.

"OK, 60" said the driver.

"You said 75," they shouted accusingly before storming off.

"It is 60," the passengers shouted out the back window, deeply involved in the drama. Eventually the couple climbed in.

I got off at the next stop, the turn-off to Althawra. My bicycle was lifted from the roof and I rode into town to be greeted by a combination of general disbelief and great excitement. With my red head scarf and sunglasses — the kind Bashar and Basel wore in their photos — I could stare at them staring at me unnoticed. The people giggled, pointed, and snorted in delight. I wanted to laugh too, but wasn't game.

Althawra means 'the revolution', and this little town was built to accommodate the dam workers and the people who were relocated when their land was flooded. I stopped for breakfast at a small café. The man treated me like a queen. He ushered away the wide-eyed boys and set the table — fresh *foul* (beans), falafel, pickles, tomato, black sweet tea and a plate of sticky fried dough rings from a nearby stall. I tried to pay but he refused to take any money.

"Are you a tourist going to see our dam? If there is anything I can do, come straight back here. You are most welcome," he told me. I was deeply embarrassed. But it happened time and time again as I was overwhelmed by the generosity of people who are among the poorest in the Middle East. He who has so little and I who have so much, I thought. Or is it the other way around?

The soldiers were reluctant to let me cycle over the dam, but were persuaded when I told them I was heading for the 12th century Jabar citadel on the north side. The little mud brick castle, perched on a rock, used to overlook the river and had just survived the creation of the lake.

"OK," said the soldiers, "but don't stop. It's forbidden."

I rode off, feeling like a spy on a bike, overwhelmed by a desire to stop and peer over one side at the unbelievely blue lake and over the other at the dam. I couldn't resist, I just had to do it. Crossing my fingers for good luck and hoping I wouldn't get caught, I got off and peered over the side. The soldiers just laughed and waved. An official walked over to me: "A bike, very good," he said beaming.

At the citadel, a sign gloatingly told me that the grandfather of the Ottoman tribe was buried there, thwarted in his ambition to enter Asia Minor. The Syrians deeply resent the long period of occupation by the Turkish Ottoman Empire, lasting from the 16th century until the end of World War II. Syria has never recognised the handing over of the city of Antioch and the port of Iskendarun to Turkey by the French in 1939. President Assad is obdurate in his demand for the return of the Golan Heights, occupied by Israel since 1967, and feels justified in keeping 35,000 troops in Lebanon which, like Palestine, used to be part of Greater Syria.

It was a pleasant cycle back to Raqqa. There was something magnificent and inspiring about the endless, brown horizon over which those armies marched. Fishing boats bobbed along the river while women hung their washing out to dry against the backdrop of Lake Assad. The schoolchildren smiled and waved at me as they ran home to their Bedouin tents and mud houses, their gardens with neat rounded walls of mud built just as the ancient city walls were thousands of years ago. Piles of brushwood lay around the village. It came from the cotton plants after the soft white cotton balls had been picked in the autumn and was used for fuel during the winter. Precious water rushed through channels and gurgled out of pipes to irrigate the fields and provide drinking water for the sheep.

"Come and talk to us," shouted two girls handling a horse and cart that was loaded with sacks of cotton. "Where do you come from? Where is your husband? Welcome, welcome."

The mood changed as I cycled into Raqqa through a wasteland of squalor. The vast, stagnant pools of water and contaminated and stinking rubbish piles where people lived was in sharp contrast to the bright future suggested by the enormous golden statue of the president which dominated a square at the entrance to the new city.

Desperate for some relief, I headed off to ancient Raqqa and rode around the substantial remains of the vast circular walls of mud which were built in the 8th century during the Abbasid period. Harun al-Rashid, of Arabian Nights fame spent his summers here. Some children ran up to me.

"A foreigner, a foreigner," they screamed. "Did you cycle all the way from England?"

In Raqqa, I stayed in a cheap dump of a hotel where everybody gathered in the central lounge which was kept warm by a huge smelly heater. My heart sank when the manager introduced his uncle who was, inevitably, an English teacher. Uncle sat down beside me and asked whether I was married and had children. He then invited me back to his house, only a few minutes away, so I could help him with some questions he had. I suggested he bring his questions to the hotel the following evening.

The next evening he was there, questions at the ready. The most important one turned out to be what was the difference between regular coffee and de-caffeinated coffee. He also wanted to know the answers to, what I thought, some rather curious questions: "Why can you not read the news on television?" and "Why can you not be Prime Minister?" I felt sorry for the bright-eyed children I'd met along the way, so thirsty for knowledge and so keen to speak English. I'm afraid I dismissed uncle rather abruptly and he took his questions to a couple of French tourists who were also staying in the hotel. I went to bed, snuggling into my pit with its traditional heavy cotton quilt — nose below the cover because of the cold.

At the Raqqa museum the next day, I realised how busy the eastern deserts of Syria once were. Every mound seemed to be able to tell a tale, or was a site where whole cities lived, flourished and died, only to be replaced by another. Syria is an archaeologists dream. A place where the experts can poke their trowels through thousands of years of history and unearth oil lamps, rings, bracelets, glass and statues of ancient gods and goddesses. I fell in love with a little statue of a naked goddess smiling gleefully as she clutched her breasts. The elderly beaming curator, who had materialised from nowhere with the key as I stood in front of the locked museum doors, pointed with relish at an old stone coffin with a 'dead person' inside. "So shall we be," he said.

I cycled out from Mansura the following day to visit an entire dead city. Resafeh, a huge walled city 20 miles south of the Euphrates is situated in the middle of the featureless desert. It was built by the Romans in the third century AD as a fort to protect against the Persians. When a Christian officer in the Roman army was horribly murdered and became a martyr and a saint, the city became a busy centre for pilgrims. It was hard to imagine as I cycled through the desert with only Bedouin tents and flocks of woolly sheep for company. The city appeared suddenly, its stone walls seemingly intact. But as you get closer they turn out to be gaping holes in them. The cathedral of St. Sergius is visible over the walls. It is an extraordinary and unexpected sight. In the 8th Century, the Omayyads, who were based in Damascus, used Resafeh as a summer palace, riding out into the desert, hawks on hand, harnesses jingling. When the Abbasids, who were based in Baghdad, took over, Resafeh was laid to waste. I tiptoed through the ornate stone gateway into a dead city of ruined churches, water cisterns, streets and ramparts and shivered at the thought of ghosts. The French couple from the hotel turned up to rescue me from my loneliness and we sat, profanely in the middle of the cathedral, eating Syrian cakes popping with honey and nuts, sweet oranges and pistachio nuts from Iran for lunch.

I cycled out of Raqqa, past the golden statue of 'god', out of town and over the river where I turned left. My goal for the day was the Byzantine fort of Halabiyeh, about 50 miles away on the Euphrates near the city of Deir Ez Zor. I was gambling on being able to find a family to stay with. The going was tough. Contrary to popular belief, cycling on excessively flat surfaces is not easy as the leg and back muscles slowly seize up with the repetitive movements. There was a prevailing wind and I hadn't eaten enough to keep my energy levels up.

I stopped to eat a *falafel* sandwich, collapsing on to a convenient low wall that belonged to the house of an extended family and was quickly surrounded by numerous children and inquisitive adults who warmly invited me inside. I was too tired to move so they brought me a long, cool glass of water. They had handsome faces with fine, strong mouths and noses. The women wore long, brightly-coloured dresses, head scarves and turbans. Veils with stars and glitter covering dark, beautiful eyes that were heavily rimmed with black kohl. Where was my husband, they asked.

The men were dignified in cloaks and long robes, their heads swathed in red and white scarves. The women exuded a heavy smell of musky perfume and I made a mental note to buy some in the Damascus *souks*. I felt scruffy by comparison.

Continuing on, with occasional glimpses of the blue river sliding through the biscuit-brown lands, I collapsed again, this time in front of a small greengrocers shop in a small town. The owner rushed home and brought back a table and chair which he solemnly placed amongst the enormous white cauliflowers, green peppers and mounds of oranges. His wife arrived with a pot of tea and a small bowl of sugar and I sat in splendid isolation on my stage, sipping my glass of tea, surrounded by an admiring audience.

The climb to the heights before Halabiyeh nearly finished me off. I was reduced to pushing the bicycle up the slopes. I was running out of water and the sun was rapidly sinking in a great ball of red. The road wound higher and higher, flattening out onto a plateau that offered marvellous views. I was balancing on the edge of the world, a small creeping thing, battling against the wind. How did you get whole armies across this land? What did you feed them on? Locust-like, they must have devastated the cultivations along the river as they tramped by. I pedalled furiously along the plateau, unable to take advantage of the downhill run because of the buffeting winds, to arrive at the turn off to Halabiyeh just as the sun was setting. The people in the corner shop offered me a sympathetic chair to fall into, administered cold water from their courtyard well and invited me in for the night.

Their extended family house was a series of large rooms constructed around a central courtyard where children, lambs, baby goats and cats skipped, played, bleated and cried. I was led off to the first room which looked as if it had just been built. The walls were bare breeze block, the electric light was rigged up from a dangling wire and mats and cushions were laid on the concrete floor. We drank glasses of tea around a central wood-burning stove. The women had strong faces and hands. One said that she was 35-years-old, had ten children and was expecting another. They were amazed when I confessed I didn't have a husband, sons or even daughters. One tiny, pretty girl said she had come from Aleppo three years ago when she married into the family. She didn't like it at all and missed the city. She had two small daughters and didn't want any more children. She was pummelling an enormous pan of dough which would be the next days bread, laboriously working in the water and kneading it with her fists.

"What a huge amount of dough," I said.

"There are a lot of us," she said, smiling slightly.

Later, her husband Mohammed, a teacher of Arabic in the local school, talked about getting more wives and having some sons, although he acknowledged his wife wouldn't like it. I wondered about the cost. He took me outside to see the 200 sheep behind a wall. "We have plenty of money," he said, but the food was the poorest I had ever come across. The evening meal was a mixture of recycled bread and something which looked like goats head but with no meat on it, just slippery rubber. Yet they had generously made me a dish of eggs as soon as I arrived.

Mohammed shook his head at the idea of people in the West living alone outside the family. Later, after I'd lost count of the number of adults and children in the various rooms, we gathered around the warm stoves, relaxing in the palpable feeling of well-being, the companionship, the sleeping babies, cradles rocking and cats asleep on the snug cotton quilts which were laid out on mattresses on the floor. All too soon it was time for bed.

The women were up at 5am the next morning to pray before starting their tasks, baking the bread, milking the animals and sweeping the floors. I felt like an indolent rich time waster as I rejected a proposal of marriage from Mohammed, said my goodbyes and cycled off down the track to the Byzantine fort of Halabiyeh that overlooks the river.

The great Palmyran queen, Zenobia, had the fort built here. It was heavily fortified by the Byzantine emperor, Justinian in the 6th century to protect against raids by the Persians. I pedalled through one gate in the huge ramparts and crossed through, among the tumbled stones inside, and shot out of the Eastern gate in a panic, overwhelmed by the weight of the past, the lost glory, the endless battles and man's capacity to build and destroy and build again. Almost opposite, on the other side of the river is another Byzantine fortification, Zalabiyeh. I cycled across the new bridge over the Euphrates, turned right and headed for Deir Ez Zor, the road that relentlessly heads south along the line of the river.

I passed through wonderful villages with neatly walled gardens where everybody offered tea and sympathy and through poorer villages where hordes of screaming children threatened to chuck stones and dogs rushed out barking furiously. I stopped to drink tea with Hassan whose sister ran the local pharmacy. He was a student at Deir Ez Zor University where he was studying to be an agricultural engineer. Syria was a poor country, he said, because the government spent everything on the army to combat the threat of Israel. He said Syrian people didn't understand why the West thought so badly of them. The Israelis would one day pay for what they had done to the Palestinians and return the Golan Heights to Syria.

It was a relief to cycle into Deir Ez Zor, the capital of eastern Syria and the heart of its oil, gas, cotton and wheat production. I visited the Armenian Church to see the museum in the crypt that was dedicated to the memory of an estimated 1.5 million Armenians who died or were murdered when they were displaced from Anatolia as the Ottoman Empire collapsed.

Some of the killings were carried out on behalf of the Ottoman Turks by the Kurds, and Turkey still refuses to acknowledge the disaster. The handsome Turkish-speaking priest sang a lament for me over the sample of human bones displayed in glass cases.

I travelled by bus out of Deir Ez Zor and south to Salihiyeh. We went through fields that were white with salt. It looked like snow. Syria is hoping a dam being constructed on a tributary of the Euphrates in the north east of the country will bring relief to farmers struggling to irrigate their crops using increasingly contaminated water from wells. The Syrians are deeply worried about massive plans by Turkey to dam the Euphrates through South-eastern Anatolia and the potential impact on the river flow through Syria.

At Salihiyeh, I left the bus and trudged through the desert towards the imposing walls of the ancient city of Dura Europos, balanced on an escarpment overhanging the river. Dura was founded by the Macedonian Greeks around 280 BC as a fortified caravan city to handle goods arriving by water. The goods were then loaded onto camels and carried over to Palmyra and the Mediterranean. This rich city was destroyed by the Persians in the middle of the third century and swallowed up by the sands. Seventeen hundred years later, after the First World War, a British soldier discovered it when he tripped over a corner of a temple. Excavations by the French and the Americans revealed that Dura Europos was a city of religious tolerance, with temples to Greek, Roman and Palmyran gods as well as Jewish and Christian places of worship, all sitting virtually side by side. The unique synagogue that was unearthed was found to be lavishly decorated in glowing colours with scenes from the Old Testament — strictly against Jewish law. It is now beautifully preserved in the museum in Damascus. The Americans took the Dura church, the earliest dated church found so far in the world, back to Yale. Many of its paintings were destroyed in transit.

I wandered around the ruins and down to the river with a group of teachers and students from a nearby town. The girls envied me for my freedom, although they were all looking forward to getting married. The men asked me whether I liked British Prime Minister Tony Blair, or Israel's former Prime Minister, Benjamin Netanyahu. They would not comment on their president, Hafiz Assad, nor the probability of his son Bashar taking over the reins of power. They would not even joke about Bashar's reported interest in computers and whether he would officially allow the use of email in Syria. Nobody discusses home politics in Syria. Ever. It was the same, to begin with, when an Iraqi picked me up outside Dura Europos to give me a lift back into Deir Ez Zor. Life in Iraq was unspeakable, he said, but Saddam Hussein was a fine man. Then he suddenly pointed to his receding greying hair; "Saddam did this to me," he said and asked if I could help him get to Britain somehow.

One of the students I met in Dura Europos rang me at my hotel that evening.

"It was so nice to meet you," she said. "We loved you very much. Please come and stay with us next time."

Back in the crush that is Damascus, I missed the Euphrates River, that enigmatic waterway that runs like a thread through history, whirling through the past, present and future. Leaders from both the West and the East would do well to spend a couple of weeks contemplating its murky waters and consider the civilisations that have risen and fallen alongside it, at what cost, and what is left of them.

Life and Death on the Nile

by Mike Gerrard

He looked like Eddie Murphy when he smiled, but Mohammed wasn't smiling now. His mother had died 12 days earlier. As the only son still living at home with his blind father, Mohammed was deeply affected by the death. "She was everything to me," he told me. "My friend, my hope, my life... everything."

Like many tourist guides in Luxor, Mohammed began as a boy leading a donkey, offering trips round the Valley of the Kings or down the banks of the Nile to those travellers wanting to see something of the real Egypt. Now he worked in partnership with my friend, Gaber, whose turquoise business card proudly announced that 'Gaber Abd-el-Rady Ahmed-el-Kawamly Renders Best Services to Tourists'.

I'd met Gaber in 1990 on my first day in Luxor. I was going to the bank to change some money and had no intention of hiring a guide, taking a ride in a horse-drawn carriage, buying a 'genuine antique from a Pharaoh's tomb' or anything else on offer. A few days later I went into a souvenir shop and was a bit taken aback when the guy behind the counter pointed to his female assistant and whispered: "You want to sleep with her?"

"Er, no thank you," I said with my best English manners, "just some postcards."

Gaber was lounging against the wall of a hotel, looking very smart in his pale blue *gallabiya* and, as expected, asked me if I wanted a guide. He was extremely polite, though not pushy like many other would-be guides, and I stopped for a chat. After reaching inside his *gallabiya* to produce his impressive business card, he handed me a testimonial letter from a Sheffield couple. They vouched for Gaber's honesty, and told about the good time he'd shown them, including hospitality at his home and a visit to a cousin's wedding.

"OK," I said, "what can you show me?" We settled for a donkey ride away from the Valley of the Kings, along the Nile to the next village, then back to Gaber's home to meet his family and have some tea. "How much?" I asked.

"Well," said Gaber, "I have to hire the donkeys and they will cost seven Egyptian pounds."

"And for you?" I asked him.

"For me," he said, "if you don't have a good time you pay nothing."

"And if I do have a good time?"

"Well," he said, with a cheeky smile, "I think I am worth two donkeys."

We were soon off across the river on a noisy, dusty local ferry, full of children and chickens and motorbikes, unshaven Egyptian men in blue or white *gallabiyas*, and black-cloaked Egyptian women, carrying bulging bags of shopping. Gaber whistled ahead to a donkey boy, who had two animals waiting by the time we reached the other side.

Gaber then took me around the villages on Luxor's West Bank, where bee-eaters sat like jewels on the telegraph wires, and pied kingfishers hovered over the Nile like the helicopters that were flying over recently invaded Kuwait. Saddam Hussein's reign of terror in the Middle East had sent Luxor's tourism figures plummeting and Gaber implored me: "Tell the people when you get home that Egypt is 1000 miles from Kuwait. It is perfectly safe here."

Despite that, visitors were down 75 per cent from their normal levels and guys like Gaber, with five children to support from his earnings as a guide, were suffering. He told me what he would like to do to Saddam, and cursed him for not being a good Muslim. "The Qur'an preaches peace," Gaber told me. "A good Muslim is a man of peace, not a man of war like this."

Further on we passed another donkey which was munching hay at the side of the track. Or rather, Gaber passed it on his donkey. My own, the sex of which I had not previously concerned myself with, began to take an interest in the feeding animal. Up top, I was unable to see what was going on below me, but it soon became obvious that my donkey was male and the tethered one was female. As my donkey advanced on the female's rear quarters. I quickly pulled back on the rope bridle. But no little bit of rope was going to stop this creature. After all, a donkey's gotta do what a donkey's gotta to do. To Gaber's horror and my embarrassment, my donkey mounted the willing female. There is only one thing you can do when you're on the back of a bonking donkey — fall off. Backwards, over the tail I went, thumping into the banks of the Nile like a sack of potatoes.

To his credit, Gaber kept a straight face and asked if I was OK. I had actually landed on my wallet, so that didn't cushion the fall much and left me with a sore hip for the next few days. It could have been worse, I could have been on the back of the female donkey. We swapped mounts and continued along the side of the Nile.

"What would you do without tourists?" I asked Gaber, when I had got over my embarrassment. "Maybe work in a factory," he told me. "My brother, he taxi driver, but he work with tourists also. Work in factory, not so healthy. Work with tourists much better. Meet people, very nice people, from England, Germany, America, Japan... everywhere. Earn more money too. If you want honey you must have money." And Gaber broke into his cackling laugh.

At the end of that first week, Gaber insisted that I should return to Luxor, and that we should occasionally exchange letters or postcards. Though Gaber spoke good English he was unable to write it, so from time to time he would dictate a letter to one of the friendlier tourists and ask them to post it to me. At the end of each one was a plea — when will we see you in Luxor again?

It took a few years but I did go back, and arranged to meet Gaber outside my hotel. I waited nervously, as I knew going back was always a gamble, but as soon as he came into view and we hugged each other, I knew I would have a good time.

Gaber took me to his village straight away. We went across the Nile on the local ferry. The rough and ready one the villagers use, not the smart tourist ferry that goes from the hotels to the magnificent tombs. My one previous trip on the tourist ferry had been a sedate experience, a quiet murmuring of polite voices, a clicking of camera shutters, a slap of suntan cream. On the local ferry there were dozens of chattering schoolchildren. The girls were like brightly coloured birds in contrast to the older ladies in their black gowns, some balancing sacks of clothes on their heads. There were cars and motor bikes, old men, young men, animals, noise, shouts, laughter, chaos — life.

We left the concrete on the East bank behind, and headed for green fields of sugar cane and clusters of mud houses on the West bank. Landing amongst brown water buffalos I walked past women in black, men in milky-blue *gallabiyas,* chickens scratching, donkeys seeking shade, palm leaves and children shouting "hello, hello, welcome".

At Gaber's house, I greeted his wife, his mother and some of his children. I gave them a portable stereo I had brought as a gift. As Arabic music blared through the small upstairs living room, I stood out on the foot-wide balcony and sipped fresh lemon juice. Below me a few women were sitting round the water pump, cleaning a mountain of pots and pans. Children stood on the springs of a bed-frame calling out 'hello' repeatedly.

Mohammed invited me to visit his house, around the corner from Gaber, when he would be receiving visitors in a few days' time and accept their condolences for the death of his mother. I told him I would be honoured to visit him. "It is the tradition," he said, "that on this day I stay in the home and receive the guests, who come from all over. Not just this village, some come from a long way away. This is the tradition in Egypt. The family is important. We share everything. We share our happiness and our sadness. If I have good news I come to tell Gaber and he is pleased with me. Now I have bad news, everyone comes to tell me they are sorry. They say not to worry."

Before visiting Mohammed, I went to see another friend from my previous trip, Captain Mahmod, who sails his felucca, the Nile King, as his father did before him. He sent his son for two cups of tea, and sat with me in the shade of his boat. "Tourism is good this year," he says. "Lots of visitors." And what do you do when it's bad, I ask him. "Sleep," he laughs.

Mahmod stood up to look for his son and noticed a friend at least 100 metres down the river. "Ahmed," he yelled with a voice that would have woken King Tut. Mahmod smiled: "Egyptian telephone".

We talked about Mohammed's mother, and I asked if I should take anything with me when I went to pay my respects. "Some tea, or maybe cigarettes. Just a little gift," he replied.

The next day I bought some cigarettes and made my way to Mohammed's house with Gabor. He welcomed me, accepted the cigarettes and hugged me like a brother. On a faded rug in a corner of the room sat two men, one of them blind like Mohammed's father. They were chanting from the Qur'an, a prayer that to me, not understanding Arabic, seemed to flow on and on like a river. It rushed, it slowed, it turned this way and that, but it never stoped. Other visitors came in, shook Mohammed's hand, left a gift, and departed. Sitting by the window, Mohammed's father fumbled for his packet of cigarettes on the sill, and shouted for a light. A small boy — in Egypt there is always a small boy to run errands, take a message, fetch a *shisha* water pipe — brought over matches and then returned to sit at the feet of the blind singer. Later he helped him stand, put his shoes on, and lead him from the house.

Mohammed brought in some meat and rice, salad and bread, all made by seemingly invisible female relatives in the kitchen. Another small boy was sent for some bottles of Coke. The mesmerising sound of the Qur'an seemed to linger in the room with the smoke, and as Mohammed sometimes gazeed in silence at nothing in particular, I sensed his mother's presence lingering there too.

The next day I left Mohammed and Gaber for a while, and went to the Deir el-Medina. My interest was aroused by the Workers Village. People come to Luxor from all over the world and marvel at the skill that went into the building of the tombs in the Valleys of the Kings and Queens, but few make it to the more humble surrounds of the workers' houses. Yet we know more about the lives of these craftsmen than we do about the Pharaohs who employed them to build their last resting places.

Most workers were literate and left records of their daily lives on fragments of limestone known as ostraca. Hundreds of these have survived alongside *papyri* and tomb inscriptions. We know the names of the workmen, the names of their wives and children. We know of their lives and their deaths, yet have no knowledge of what happened at a royal funeral.

The men would work for eight days, then take two days off. From the Deir el-Medina, it was only a short walk over a hill to the Valley of the Kings, and the path the men took can still be followed today. Some sources say they did not return each evening, but stayed overnight near the tombs in makeshift huts. Not so, said my own guide to the village, Abdullah Abdullah. I'd wondered if it was an extravagance to hire a guide for myself, but a morning with Abdullah cost me only five Egyptian Pounds more than a packaged tour to the tombs with a coachful of other people and all the restrictions that imposes.

"Some people used to think that the workers would stay at the tombs each night," Abdullah told me, his voice a deep rumble like an earth tremor. "The story is then repeated from book to book, but it is not true. Do you think you could stop an Egyptian man from spending the night with his wife and his family, when they are only a short walk away? No. The family life was as important then as it is today, and the men returned home to eat with their family and relax, just like the men do today."

The working day began about 8am with a four-hour shift. After a break for lunch in the midday heat, another four-hour shift would follow. Each tomb had a Scribe responsible for keeping an attendance register. Absences are recorded for eye diseases and scorpion bites. During the reign of Ramases II it is recorded that a worker named Neferabu was away for a time embalming his brother, while another, Hehnekhu, was bandaging the body of his mother. One man took a day off to build his house, another because of a row with his wife.

"And there is also the story," said Abdullah, "of the man who was absent due to the funeral of his mother. Later he was absent again for the same reason, so we wonder how many mothers he had."

One wife was the norm for Egyptian workers at that time, but death or divorce would leave a man or woman free to marry again. If a man divorced his wife on any ground other than adultery, he was obliged to make some kind of settlement to her, perhaps up to one-third of the marital property. The first recorded strikes took place here, when workmen downed tools if their wages were late. There was no money, but payment was made in grain, beer, fish, vegetables, water, wood, pottery, cakes and dates. Oil, salt, meat and clothes were also occasionally made available.

Children's toys have survived, while the Turin Erotic Papyrus from this village shows that adults had their own amusements. Family life could be, as now, full of strife. A workman named Menna had a son, Merysakhmet, who had arguments at work, was involved in a court case over some stolen property, ran away from home and wandered around Egypt, and was accused of sleeping with a fellow workman's wife.

As Abdullah showed me around the site, sharing his immense knowledge with me, a French tour group arrived in a coach. One fat, balding man, inappropriately dressed in shorts, walked through the remains of the houses despite warning signs telling people to keep out to avoid damaging the ruins, which are still being excavated.

"Excuse me," Abdullah shouted to him, "but you must go round the outside."

"Pah!" the man said, dismissing Abdullah with a wave of his hand, as if he were of no consequence.

"Excuse me," Abdullah said again, still polite, "but you may damage the buildings. It is forbidden to walk through there."

"I want to get to the tomb," the man said, "and this is the quickest way."

"If you want to see the tombs," Abdullah pointed out, "you must first buy a ticket, and the ticket office is over here."

Forced to retreat, the Frenchman shouted: "Huh, Egypt! Money-money-money, pay-pay-pay."

"So," said Abdullah with a sly smile, "it is free to climb the Eiffel Tower now, is it?"

A few days later I went for a walk with Gaber around his village, and into the pottery shops, where we were welcomed with cups of tea and not pressured to buy anything. The men smoked lazily, shafts of sunlight came through the doors and windows and lit up shelves filled with pots and plates. These modern artisans working not for the Pharaohs but for tourists. After a coach party left, I asked Gaber to teach me how to haggle in true Egyptian style. He leapt up, delighted, and told his friend the shop-owner what I wanted. They both laughed, and the pantomime started.

Gaber walked slowly round the store, picking up pots, taking a look, putting them down again. The owner followed him, smiling, pointing to a few items. "Very nice," he said, "special price today." Gaber picked up a little statuette of an Egyptian cat.

"And how much is this?"

"A hundred Egyptian pounds," the owner said.

Gaber staggered back in horror. "One hundred? Is much too much. Is no good quality." He put the cat back and walked on.

"If you like the cat," the owner said, "you could have it for 90."

"No, no," said Gaber, "is too much. Maybe is worth 20."

Now it was the owner's turn to look stunned. "Twenty?" he said. "Twenty? This finest carving, look at details, is beautiful cat, take long time to make. Maybe I could let you have it for 80."

"Still too much," Gaber insisted. "I would not pay more than 30 for it."

"Seventy, this my lowest price."

"Forty,"said Gaber, "and not one pound more."

"Sixty, and not one pound less."

"Fifty," offered Gaber, and they slapped each other's hands and shook on it, laughing.

"And perhaps you have a little gift for me, like this one," Gaber said, picking up a tiny carving and including it in the bargain.

"That is how you haggle," Gaber told me, as we settled down with our cups of tea.

I learnt much more about everyday Egyptian life from Gaber, things that no amount of time spent in tourist hotels would have shown me. Like baksheesh, which some visitors regard as a curse, forever being expected to hand over tips to people.

"*Baksheesh*," said Gaber, "is our way of life. It is not just trying to get money out of tourists. Egyptian people pay *baksheesh* all the time. If someone does something for you, then you pay them a little something. It is a way of spreading money around, from the rich people to the poor people. It is our tradition, yes. So when tourists complain about it, they are complaining about our way of doing things, which is not right. If someone just asks you for money then that is just begging. If they are a beggar and in need of money then the Qur'an says you should help them. If it is just someone passing you in the street and they ask you for *baksheesh*, then you don't have to give it."

I returned that night through the narrow streets of Gaber's village, for a final meal with his family. He'd invited his neighbour and some other musicians to play for me, one with a drum and the other two on pipes made from simple pieces of metal with a few finger holes drilled into them. They sat in their best *gellabiyas*, with dignified faces, and produced a series of infectious tunes — the thump of the drum, the wail of the pipes.

Gaber's nine-year-old daughter, Asma, tied a scarf around her hips and flicked her way round the room, her sinuous fingers swaying like snakes to the sound of the pipes. She pulled me up and tied the scarf around me, and I tried to learn the hip-flicking steps, encouraged by Asma's young brothers, Mohammed and Mustafa. The older Ibrahim was shyer, while Gaber's studious eldest child, 16-year-old Maria, was in another room trying to do her homework.

The other Mohammed was there too, Eddie Murphy, encouraging the musicians to play faster and faster, clapping, his hands gesturing for more, like a demented band-leader. Half the village seemed to be in Gaber's front room, sharing the joy just as they had previously shared Mohammed's sorrow.

Before I left for my final ferry ride back to the 'civilised' side of the river and Luxor, Gaber weighed me down with gifts to take back to England; dozens of little lemons, peanuts, cumin and coriander, and packets of carcadet with which they made a tea I'd admired when we visited his brother. "This is the best," said Gaber. "This from Aswan. Very good carcadet."

Gaber and Mohammed walked with me down to the ferry, as Egyptian hospitality demands. The children tagged along carrying my presents in plastic bags. Little Mustafa, just eight, insisted on lugging my camera case, almost as heavy as he was. His cheeky face reminded me of a few days earlier when Gaber had been late to meet me so we could look round the market together.

"I so sorry," he said. "My wife is visiting her brother, and I have to see to the children. Mustafa is very naughty today, he would not go to school. First he cannot find his pen, then he cannot find his book, then he cannot find his shoes. I find his pen and his books outside the window, I find his shoes hidden under the bed. Is it the same in your country when children do not want to go to school?"

They saw me board the ferry, the lights of Luxor waiting at the far side of the now-black river. The captain finished his cigarette and climbed on board. The boat began to rumble and move away from the bank. We waved goodbye, till next time, and then Mohammed ran back down to the boat and shouted to me.

"Be careful when you get off at the other side," he said. "Wait for the boat to reach the bank properly. Don't jump like the Egyptian men do."

"OK," I said, "I'll be careful," thinking how fussy Mohammed can sometimes be. As the boat pulled away, and pulled me away from my friends with a wrench I could feel, I suddenly remembered why Mohammed had run back to the boat. When I'd asked Captain Mahmod what to take to the house, I'd also asked him how Mohammed's mother had died, not wanting to ask Mohammed himself. She was going to catch the ferry one day, Mahmod told me, walking down the dusty slope to the dock. Just as the boat was drawing in she lost her footing, slipped between the boat and the dock and was crushed.

Every day Mohammed must catch that same ferry, crossing the river to meet the tourists who are looking for guides. And every day he'll greet them with his Eddie Murphy smile.

Aromatic Oman

by Maria Golia

A gracious Indian couple were hosting the gathering, members of a merchant family established in Oman for over a century. The guests were representative of Omani culture and society: Zanzibari Omani entrepreneurs sipping whisky and soda, former British officers with their trophy wives and a variety of expats on missions from jobs in Burma, Malaysia and Brunei. We ate at large round tables set out on the lawn beside a swimming pool. The air was hot and blowing like an oven, the Indian food delicious, the wine French and well chilled. I flirted casually with a very tall Germanic type on my left whose arm wore a rather offensive gash held together by bits of brave suture. "Rafting in Uganda." He explained smugly.

Suddenly, as I reached for my goblet something crossed my field of vision. I felt rather than saw it alight on my *décollet* like a brooch; it was about the size and texture of a flying baby armadillo. I froze. Its femurs scratched my bosom and it was gone before I could identify it and perhaps scream. The lady on my right noted my confusion and comforted me by saying, "Never mind my dear, its locust season." I was still used to Cairo standard: the party had begun early and ended with a mass exodus around midnight. I was told that this was standard procedure since most of the guests held positions they took very seriously. One of them was the gentleman who owned the hotel where I was staying. He offered to take me to his ancestral home the next day and I readily agreed.

My host belonged to one of the wealthiest families in Oman that hailed from the ancient port town of Sur some 150 kilometers as the crow flies from Muscat on the north coast. As we drove he told me that the Suris were seafarers who sailed as far as China. Famed and feared for their fierce independence, they were wealthy before the 'oil rich' through trade, a euphemism I suspected, for smuggling and piracy. It took the Sultan twenty-three years after taking power to visit Sur. The Suris were slighted and there is no mosque bearing his name in the town.

We approached Sur on the dramatic coastal track from Ras al Hadd. On the road, at the entrance of every small village stand sculptures of towers and ships, the 'yin and yang' of Oman. Ras al Hadd, the most easterly point in Arabia, is a millennial nesting grounds for huge turtles, one of many conservationist zones. Environmentally speaking, Oman is highly advanced; the Sultans passion for beauty translates into laws protecting every biome and rare species; whales, dolphins, a host of coral and its inhabitants; oryx, ibex, gazelle, mountain goats and wildcats, scores of astonishing snakes and birds.

Sur is thought by some to be the first home of the Phoenician sailors. They still build their dhows using seven kinds of wood from the interior and India. The builders use no measuring tools other than their palms and the length of their pace. At dawn I went to the bay where the fisherman bring in their haul, mostly tuna and shark caught practically by hand. The fishermen butchered the still quivering catch with precise strokes of the knives they carry stuck in their belts, and I ate 'sushi' for breakfast.

We drove back on an inland route that skirts the Wahiba sands. The desert invades the highway so I stopped to take a walk over the low rolling pinkish coloured dunes that were covered with snake tracks. The evening found me back in Muscat, renewed. The feast was coming and it seemed propitious to plot a temporary escape. I made a few more contact calls and headed south, to Salalah.

★ ★ ★ ★ ★

My journey had begun on a white-hot airless day, when I had sat facing my computer screen blankly. The chorus of car horns that forms the soundtrack of life in Downtown Cairo built to a frenzied crescendo. I needed a shower and shed my clothes whilst padding to the bathroom where I opened the faucet and stood expectantly. A series of rust-coloured spurts of lukewarm sludge spat out of the showerhead, then stopped abruptly. I sat down on the bathtub and decided I had had enough and wanted to get out.

Books have a malignant influence on my susceptible psyche. Someone had just given me a copy of Jan Morris' 'Sultan in Oman' and I dug up my copies of Lawrence's 'Seven Pillars of Wisdom' and Thesiger's 'Arabian Sands'. The damage was done. I began to fancy myself sitting in a starlit desert camp strewn with silk carpets reciting spontaneous verse for a handsome turbaned sovereign. He would nod benevolently and fill my mouth with pieces of gold. I would fall asleep in breezy filigreed pavilions to the song of nightingales. I am a hopeless albeit practical romantic. One month later I was on my way to Oman.

I was to stay at the Holiday Inn, the least pretentious of Muscats five-star lodgings. Travelling ostensibly for business, I could not afford the negative effects of cheap digs on my corporate image. A car manned by two solicitous Indians was waiting for me at the airport. I settled in and sighed with contentment. The purple mountains of Muscat sizzled in the late afternoon heat. Ribbons of perfect road bisect them, curving artfully to reveal vistas of a placid tanker-dotted Gulf. There was virtually no sound except for the occasional cry of a strange bird or the whirr of an insect. The mosques were conspicuously soft-spoken. No one walked on the beautifully groomed streets: the glare and blare of Cairo was momentarily forgotten.

Tooling along Muscats manicured roads, I caught sight of a gazelle and an instant later realised it was just an authentically coloured model. These animal statues dot the rocky masses around town like forgotten toys, some small, some larger than life. Clusters of low white buildings lay at the throat of the mountains like pearl necklaces. Their facades all bear tribute to tradition: pointed arches, domes clad in lapis-blue and watertowers crenellated like mediaeval turrets. My first impression of the capital of Oman was Beverly Hills meets the 'Prisoner of Zenda'.

I am a city creature, but the most fantastic aspect of this remote realm was clear at a glance: Omans natural beauty is awesome. There is a stunning, nearly untouched coastline 1700 kilometres long washed by the Arabian Sea and the Indian Ocean; the Jebel Akhdar sprinkled with oases in the north; another mountain range in the south touched by the monsoons and the orange-pink Wahiba Sands and the pale towering dunes of the Rub al Khali. I vowed to finish my business and explore as quickly as possible. Over the next two weeks I penetrated a number of government offices and met the *créme de la créme* of Omani entrepreneurs. Along the way the quirky character of the sultanate gradually revealed itself.

The Omanis have style. The men, almost without exception, wear traditional dress: *disdashas* of a marvellous polished cotton with a longish tassel to the right of the lightly embroidered neckline, and *kummas*, jaunty pill-box hats decorated in arabesque. They perch or indent them variously atop their heads as a reflection of individuality. The women, well, there weren't any. The Omanis air of refinement is enhanced by their passion for scent and an informed tradition of its properties, from the medicinal to the intoxicating.

Omanis are like mobile air-fresheners. They anoint themselves with subtle essential oils that bloom in the heat and their clothing is fumigated with fragrant and costly shards of aud, the bark of a dead Cambodian tree. I was told that the tassel on their *dishdashas* is designed to be dipped by the wearer into his wifes perfume bottle so that throughout the day he can refresh himself by lifting it to his nose. Just about everyone, incidentally, is married. The desert and sea-washed air carries the sanctifying scent of native frankincense wafting in homes, offices, *souks* and ministries. If there were an award for the worlds sweetest-smelling country, Oman would win hands down.

In my daily rounds of the capital I could however barely find one Omani who was not umbilically attached to his cellular phones. They engage in lengthy conversations while ostensibly holding meetings with you. In restaurants it is not uncommon to see two people facing each other both blithely conversing with absent friends. Omanis drive to their ministry jobs in attractive but unpretentious vehicles chattering away while wearing regulation earphones, so that both hands remain obediently on the wheel. Omanis are refreshingly punctual. In fact, the work ethic is remarkable if only for the fact that unlike their richer gulf neighbours Omanis actually do work. There is a great push towards Omanisation to eliminate the ex-pat presence in the country. Of the 2.5 million inhabitants, around 500,000 are foreigners, mostly Indians, Pakistanis and Bangladeshis, they helped build the country, its wonderful roads and excellent infrastructure.

Indians also hold key positions in Omani-owned businesses and are in large part responsible for the Omani newspapers. Their front pages carry two crucial daily features; royal decrees in the upper left-hand column and the prices of oil where most other papers would the weather: Omani Crude, Arabian Light, Arabian Heavy and West Texas Intermediate. This is the way the days are measured, and the prices lately are alarmingly low. Accordingly government spending has come to a halt.

Everything in Oman was built according to the priorities and aesthetic dictates of the Sandhurst-educated Sultan since he deposed his ultra-reactionary father in 1973. At that time there was one hospital and three schools in all of Oman. Today the signs of well being and tasteful opulence are in abundant evidence. The ministries are a series of seaside palaces; all grey pile-carpeted affairs that resemble health spas during the off-season, luxurious but semi-deserted. Carpet shampooing, I surmised, must be a big business in Muscat. The facades of banks resemble post-modern temples; jewel-like mosques sparkle with gilt and Italian marbles. There are marvellous government financed art galleries, parks and promenades. The supermarkets are so well-stocked with international delicacies and pristine clean produce that they made me gasp; accustomed as I was to sorting through muddied vegetables in the back of a pick-up truck on one of Cairos cluttered street corners.

Visiting Muscats five-star hotels offers the uplifting equivalent of perusing historic monuments in other countries. The El Bustan Palace has a foyer with a volume of space that rivals St. Peters Cathedral. The Hyatt Regency was financed by a Yemeni prince for a kings ransom and is appropriately lavish and sophisticated. The immense lobby houses a bronze statue of an Arab horseman holding a falcon on his arm that makes a full silent circuit on its pedestal once an hour.

I discovered that the Sultanate is a small, royal world of possession in great measure, at odds with the occasional petulance of its subjects. Omanis can be heard to lament without malice but with the slightest hint of a whine that "we are not rich like the Saudis, or the Kuwaitis". When ten cars get together they call it a traffic jam. The people are well mannered and discreetly hospitable. When you warm them up a bit they drop some of that Persian reserve, but not too much. Living in a benevolent sultanate they have rules to obey. Significantly, dancing is allowed only in certain seedy establishments. Infractions like fighting and drinking to excess are punished with six-month jail stints. One Omani told me, "We are very nice people, don't you think?"

"Very nice" I agreed.

"If we are not nice we go to jail. If we go to jail we lose our jobs. If we lose our jobs we are finished," he concluded philosophically.

Oman is an insular country in some ways and people are addicted to CNN. There aren't many single American women traipsing about this stretch of the Tropic of Cancer and I often felt that they viewed me as a sort of loose woman. The Clinton scandal was dominating the news and I perceived a hint of moral snobbery towards my nationality and a sly appraisal, as if they considered Monica Lewinsky an advertisement for American womanhood, and myself, a sample of the brand. Luckily I had the phone number of an Egyptian friend who offered to take me sightseeing.

Old Muscat has a small harbour where the Sultan's yacht bobs regally. There is a *souq* dominated by Indian merchants and a few tangled streets melded onto the foot of the mountains that rise unexpectedly within the town. Along the corniche are panels featuring large replicas of extravagant native birds. Muscat is at its evocative best in the royal enclosure, open to all at any hour to stroll between the graceful austere buildings of the diwan. The scale is human, albeit royal human, lit like a stage-set and practically deserted with hardly even a guard. Grey masses of rock drop into the sea beside the pistil and stamen shaped entrance to His Majesty's abode. A deep peace pervades, and the fortresses of Merani and Jalali stand sentry. The night is scented with flowers from his gardens, varieties of frangipani and jasmine, a cloying scent sharpened by a note of brine.

Stories circulate about the man who likes to drive and was behind the wheel when a collision caused the death of his passenger, a dear friend. Following the incident he issued an edict regarding the succession, yet in the absence of a direct heir the future is uncertain at best. Sultan Qaboos is what you might call a hard act to follow. My companion said, "I know people who are close to him. They tell me his presence is intoxicating." My visions revived of sitting Shaharazade-like at his feet cooking up poetic prose to encourage the nascent tourism industry. I promised once more to crack the nut of Omani formality and insinuate myself into the local writing scene.

* * * * *

An hour by plane from Muscat, Salalah has a tropical air, with its coconut groves and stands selling the fruit with straws to drink the water. The sea is a gorgeous, glassy green wall of water. I saw my first dolphin from a beachside hotel window, a mysterious black movement in the waves. In July and August the monsoon comes to this region of Dhofar, a thick mist that obscures the sun and turns the hills emerald green. Jersey cows pasture here, as incongruous as the landscape that just past the hills turns to stark desert once again.

For now the jebel above Salalah is covered with brownish fuzz and twisted trees, and hundreds of camels grazing. After the monsoon they swarm the hills in their tens of thousands and paradoxically become Omans only endangered species.

"They kill people," said my chauffeur meaning the danger they were to drivers. "We are thinking of solutions. Perhaps we will put them in cans and export them." Apparently camels are high in protein — so much for the so-called ships of the desert.

Much of Omans history is linked to the frankincense that these camels carried through the desert. Used in religious rites all over the world since antiquity, frankincense made fortunes. It travelled as far afield as Rome and demand was such that its cost per gram has been recorded as equivalent to about £300 today. One of the main sites along this trade route and one of the most profitable in the ancient world is a city called Shisur, often known as Ubar or the 'Atlantis of the Sands'.

For many centuries the city had been lost below the dunes that move like waves with the wind and the seasons around the Rub al Khali, or Empty Quarter, until it was rediscovered by a team led by Ranulph Fiennes in 1992. Many had believed it was a myth, but I befriended an archaeologist who assisted Juris Zarins, the Neolithic Arabian archaeologist who excavated Shisur. About 180 kilometres from Salalah lie the ruins of a three thousand-year-old citadel standing on a 300-metre high outcropping just above access to an aquifer, the last water source and trading place for caravans embarking across the vast distance of the Empty Quarter with their cargoes of spices and incense bound for the West coast of Arabia and Europe.

Shisur lies on the fringes of the largest sand desert in the world, a local Bedouin took me in, regaling me with stories of his fathers crossings and celestial navigation. The sand is the palest beige, soft as velvet, and the dunes immense. Night falls and the beauty of the place goes straight to the soul like a draught of immortality. The desert has an immediacy that absorbs pasts and futures, whittling it all down to a grain of now. I learned that the sand is treacherous, even for the most experienced of drivers. There was a moment that I imagined we were lost and the notion produced a new sensation in me, something past erotic. It was the briefest taste, but I savoured the power that drove my heroes — Lawrence, Thesiger and Doughty — to endure hardship in order to drink of it more fully.

Back in Salalah I toured the Royal Razat Farm, a 450 hectare establishment belonging to the Sultan and supplying his tables. Fields of maize, papaya, coconut, banana and bread fruit groves, feathery henna trees, and more Jersey cows grazing on pasture kept green by a 24-hour technological mist, a stable of splendid horses, a small aviary and an oddity, even a kennel for the royal dogs. Queen Elizabeth had the singular idea of rewarding this devout Muslims allegiance with a pair of terriers — dirty animals according to Islamic tradition.

"The Arabic language started in Dhofar," said Susan, a Swedish woman who ran the hotel where I was staying. She suggested I meet a man who had discovered cave paintings in the hills surrounding Salalah. He based his theory of the origins of Arabic on the ancient cave-drawings that are accompanied by strings of symbols that he theorises were an early alphabet. He said that the geometric paintings were maps describing the location of water sources and pastureland in the largely barren mountains. But to me the drawings looked totemic, smacking of some ritual magic. A tribe called the Jeballi live in the mountains and can occasionally be seen on shopping excursions in town or driving their camel herds along its outskirts. Naked from the waist up except for cartridge belts, they carry rifles and wear indigo coloured wraps that dye their bodies a deep bluish purple. The scholar man belonged to the tribe.

I had a phone number for another local personality who was a close relation of the governor of the province. Ever ambitious to establish contact with Omani dignitaries I gave him a call. He wasn't the least reticent about a meeting and went so far as to suggest that we rendezvous in my hotel.

"It is the feast and everything is closed" he explained. "Perhaps I can bring along some dinner from my club. And what do you drink? Myself it is vodka." I was slightly taken aback, since aside from the Holiday Inn, Salalah was dry and its natives abstemious. I happened to have a salon in my beach villa and suggested that if he wouldnt mind my inviting my Swedish hostess, then that would be fine. He promised to come at eight.

Susan agreed to chaperon and Salem arrived punctually with several foil-wrapped packages and a bottle of Absolute vodka. We made each others acquaintance while Salem extolled the virtues of his favourite cocktail. "Vodka and coconut water" he said smacking his lips. "It is odourless. It does not produce hangover and it is more hydrating than water itself. Also it is helpful for the digestion." We spent the evening drinking and chatting. Salem had a condescending way about him, a side effect of his highborn position in Salalah. Every time Susan or I mentioned something lacking in our lives, he promised to procure it the next day: my sunglasses lost in a rogue wave while swimming; Susans problem with parking at the airport; information regarding the caloric content of coconut water.

Salem wore a huge diamond ring set in white metal on his little finger and a watch whose face featured a mini-Oman set in diamond chips. He said they were gifts from the Sultan but I couldn't help thinking they looked suspiciously fake. "He is a very generous man if you show him what you can do" he told us. Salem is a champion dart-player.

He said he had invested in abalone farming, one of the biggest new ventures in Salalah. The Omanis hired the Japanese, to profit from their expertise in cultivating the lucrative shellfish. Both parties are enthusiastic about the aphrodisiac properties of the molluscs and the conversation degenerated as Salem began to describe them. I managed to veer the discussion towards the subject of family life. He had three children and he passed along His Majesty's words of wisdom on family planning. "A car has only five seats because a perfect family has three children and two adults." We nodded in agreement with this implacable logic while dining on lobster thermidor.

I awoke early the next morning and opened the window facing the sea. Just then a mounted brigade of royal guards galloped past, looking ghost-like in the mist, the hooves of the animals muffled in the sand. I walked down to the beach once more, hoping to catch sight of a dolphin and to say so-long to Salalah and the Indian Ocean that I would soon exchange for my corner of the Egyptian Sahara.

The taste of India is strong in Salalah especially at a popular restaurant called Hassan Thabit. It has a series of alcoves with sliding doors for men who wish to seclude their women while supping on dishes like chicken lollipop and cream of princess soup. I enjoyed these delicacies on my last evening before Susan drove me to the bus station. We crossed Oman throughout the long cool desert night and dawn found me once again in Muscat. I checked back into the Holiday Inn and the man in the reception desks told me I had several messages. I leafed through them distractedly, worn out from my journey but one of them caught my eye. It said "Heard you are writing. Please call Mr. Sultan."

Coincidentally, one of the most influential family businesses in the sultanate carried the surname of Sultan. I met that day with the elder brother-in-charge who commissioned me to write a profile of his 125-year-old shipping company. I'd wished for a Sultan and I got one of sorts. As for HM, I would just have to keep trying. I had travelled to Oman in search of the last stronghold of the Arabian Nights and its polished exotica did not entirely disappoint me. Oman's tastes are rare and fine and its beauty penetrates.

Arriving in Cairo the sky was brownish grey and in the frustrated heat of the late afternoon the urban sprawl resembled nothing so much as a tattered dishrag. But as I entered the womb of the city, passing the grove of minarets of Fatamid Cairo, my spirits lifted. The mad bustle of downtown was a welcome contrast to Omans austerity. Cairo smelled like a burnt offering, mingling kebab smoke with exhaust fumes and the dust of ages. I sniffed the air appreciatively. This, at least, seemed real.

Easter in the Lebanon

by Tom Perry

"Joyeaux Pacques, Joyeaux Pacques," came the greeting from the elderly lady as she emerged from the little stone house. "Christ is risen, Christ is risen," came the reply from Selwa as the bells tolled in agreement from the proliferation of local churches. Another villager offered congratulations as she made her way to the little white church that clung precariously to the hillside, incense burner in one hand and menacing looking candle stick in the other.

It was noon on Easter Saturday and for the Catholic and Christian Maronite population of the little village of Ghazir it was time to celebrate Jesus' resurrection. I gazed up the mountain, admiring the scene whilst trying to count the ornate white-washed spires whose bells seemed to get louder and louder. Pointing to a spot on the mountain, my guide called out: "There Thomas, can you see our home?"

It was easy to spot the little house where I had spent the previous few days. The uninhabited first floor turret sat atop the thick stone walls, flagging the position of the fortress-like abode. Like the rest of the homes in Ghazir, the building seemed to nestle into the mountain, sitting comfortably amidst the orange trees and terraced gardens.

We'd walked down the winding mountain passes into the village that morning, attracting curious stares from locals who rarely walk anywhere.

Amine, my hosts' five-year-old son, skipped along the narrow grass verges, picking spring flowers that sprouted from the rocks. Brandishing flowers in one hand and holding my arm in his other, Amine led me towards the shrine in the yard of his French school. He dutifully approached the rock cave and stood on tiptoe so he could place the flowers at the feet of a figure of the Virgin Mary.

Such shrines abound in the village, and I'd already spotted a multitude of roadside cabinets containing candles, flowers and figurines of Mary and Jesus. That morning I'd taken a stroll up the mountain to walk amongst the pine tree-covered slopes and take in the fresh air. Feeling sure I would come across a shrine at some point, I was not surprised when I rounded a bend and bumped into a large statue of Christ hidden behind a conifer. There were no crash barriers on the winding passes, and one could not help feeling that the proliferation of shrines were designed to act as a substitute, providing divine guidance to the locals who careered down the mountain road with scant regard for their safety.

After finishing his prayer, Amine took my hand again, leading me from the school yard and back onto the village high street where we continued our descent. Passing by the lowered doors of the stone dwellings, Selwa told me that 17th Century builders kept the entrances low to deter Ottoman overlords from entering on horseback.

Suddenly a muddy old BMW skidded to a halt in the middle of the road. The smiling face of Jamal, Selwa's brother, appeared from behind the dusty windscreen. A blaring orchestra of car horns quickly followed as furious drivers behind him vented their anger as they were forced to detour through the adjacent petrol station forecourt.

I had been planning to take the bus from the nearby town of Jounieh to Beirut, but my surrogate family firmly insisted that they take me by car. As they loaded my bags into the boot, a sudden commotion erupted outside a nearby shop as two butchers attempted to winch a live cow off the pavement. Their boss was gesticulating wildly, trying to redirect the efforts of his employees who were failing their task miserably, the cow making a frantic bid for freedom as the ropes slipped from its feet.

As we got closer to the coast the buildings increased in height and vulgarity, marking the beginning of the seaside district of Jounieh. Like Ghazir, Jounieh is predominantly a Christian town. Its rapid and unfortunate development from fishing port to monstrous concrete jungle can partly be attributed to Christian migration from Beirut after the outbreak of civil war in

1975. A series of magnificent cathedrals and statues on the mountains that surround Jounieh alert the visitor to its resident's religious beliefs. I could make out the sweeping lines of the space-age Maronite basilica at Harissa, directly behind a 13-tonne statue of the Virgin Mary. Like Amine's school, the gleaming white statue had been imported from France in the 19th Century, alluding to the cultural ties that have made such a huge impact in the area.

The link between the Maronites and Europeans was first made in the 12th Century when the advancing crusaders made allies of Mount Lebanon's Maronite Christian community. Using their extensive local knowledge, the Maronites' guided the Crusaders through the valleys of the Mount Lebanon range. Approximately 800 years later another European was being guided through a mountain village, although my intentions were less hostile — and my Maronite guide was less than three feet tall. Links between the foreign army and the Maronites were confirmed when the Maronites accepted the religious authority of the Pope and became part of the Catholic Church — the church they still belong to today. The Maronite community developed a particularly strong relationship with the French, whose cultural influence grew over the community during the 19th Century.

From the coastal highway I could see thick grey clouds gathering over the mountain, filling the valleys with a misty haze that crept towards the shore. The basilica at Harissa was slowly obscured as the elements threatened a repeat of the thunder and lightning that had attacked the area on the previous two nights.

The heavy storms had fed the muddy waters of the Nahr al-Kalb, (Dog River), which were flowing rapidly as we left Jounieh behind us on the road south to Beirut. The rocky headland at the mouth of the river has been made famous by guide books because of carvings by various marauding armies that stormed through the area over the centuries. I had visited the valley earlier in the week to see carvings left by ancient Assyrians, Greeks and Egyptians. Of more contemporary interest, I noticed the façade left by the French army after they arrived in 1920 to take possession of the region which they then moulded into Syria and Lebanon. Climbing the stairs which had been chiselled into the headland, I came across the weathered image of a roughly carved triangular cedar tree. A passer-by told me it was the symbol of the Maronite-led Kata'ib and had been carved during the war. Otherwise known as the Phalange, the Kata'ib was one of the Lebanese militias that fought with each other after the outbreak of hostilities in 1975. On top of the cliff I found a trench and imagined the Phalangists firing at the enemy as they approached Jounieh from the coastal road below. The inscriptions made by the armies at the Dog River boasted of military triumph. However, none of Lebanon's militias scored a decisive victory over their rivals and it seemed ironic that the militia men carved their emblem on the rock face at Nahr al-Kalb.

Rounding the headland, we passed a final statue of Christ, arms outstretched as he balanced precariously on the pine-green mountain summit. The radio was broadcasting haunting Easter hymns sung by the national heroine Fayrouz. With the Easter celebrations in Ghazir reaching a climax, it seemed an odd time to leave. However I was heading to Beirut to spend Easter with Greek Orthodox Christians whose celebrations ran seven days behind those in Ghazir and Jounieh. The calendar confusion — which dates back to the 16th Century — seemed a little baffling, but nowhere in the world are the historic fractures in the Christian church more graphically on display than in modern-day Lebanon and Syria. In Lebanon there are around 10 denominations of Christianity whose adherents follow either Protestantism, Catholicism, Eastern Orthodoxy or Oriental Orthodoxy.

Having driven through the outskirts of Beirut, we arrived on the Corniche Mazraa and took our place in the queue of traffic crawling down the bustling road. Sporadic car horn bursts cut through the continual drone of engine noise. On the central reservation stood a grey-suited policeman with the hopeless task of organising the surrounding chaos.

Beirut buzzes with all the vibrancy of any major city, so coming to the capital from a sleepy mountain village, I was bound to notice many contrasts. But as I looked up the Corniche, the most obvious difference was immediately clear. I had not seen a single head scarf or mosque in Ghazir or Jounieh, but the scene on the Corniche immediately rung with an Islamic tone. On the brow of the hill the gleaming white minaret of the Abd al-Nasser mosque reached into the sky; on the pavement women in *Hijab* were strolling in and out of the shops. The side streets were filled with colour and decorated for the second major Muslim festival of the year; *Eid al-Adha*. Bright green and red ribbons were tied from apartment balconies to the street lamps below, adding a vivid burst of colour to the streets of Mazraa. Spectacular bunting fluttered in the gentle Beirut spring breeze, honouring the local Muslims who were returning from pilgrimage to Mecca.

It seemed ironic that I was coming here to spend Easter with Christians. The war in Lebanon lasted somewhere between 17 and 19 years although the locals have rounded this figure up to 20. During this period the western half of Beirut had been almost exclusively Muslim and the eastern half mainly Christian. Beirut was divided by the infamous 'Green Line', across which the militias fought fierce gun battles. Sniping, kidnapping and shelling encouraged much of the city's population to move from their homes to sectarian ghettos under the control of militias who claimed to represent their interests. Some of the worst fighting took place in the late 1980s between rival Christian forces. The war also had an international dimension, involving Israel, Syria, the PLO and the Superpowers, all of whom played crucial roles in a conflict which is often wrongly perceived as a simple Christian-Muslim struggle.

Turning off the Corniche into a maze of narrow streets, my thoughts turned to my late aunt who spent the war in her ageing family home amidst a set of apartment blocks in West Beirut. As Jamal eased his way through the double-parked cars, I spotted the break in the line of tower blocks which told me we had arrived at Aunt Maggie's house. I was greeted by a blaze of yellow and purple foliage that had grown over the front of the building, successfully hiding its existence. The heavy steel gate groaned as its rusting hinges grudgingly admitted entrance to the barren garden. The slatted wooden shutters had been stripped of their paint by decades of wear, and the rainfall had proved too much for the guttering which swung, defeated, from the lintel. Inside, time had stood still. A wrought iron chandelier hung precariously from the ceiling, illuminating black and white portraits of the family. In one corner of the room hung an arrangement of Christian icons and a dusty old incense burner.

The timeless spirit of the house somehow subsumed any sense of decay. But how could I even think the house had been neglected when the front wall still bore shrapnel scars from the war? It was remarkable that the house was standing at all. I guessed that the little villa had had a few scrapes — a hunch that was confirmed when my grandmother produced two mortars from the saucepan cupboard. "I was cleaning when I found them in the kitchen. I expect Maggie found them in the garden and kept them. I wasn't sure if they were safe so I asked the colonel to come and look at them. He said they had been fired." The news was a welcome relief as I examined the gruesome-shaped pieces of metal, still containing the explosive shells which had projected them over the surrounding tower blocks and into the back garden.

The Corniche Mazraa was dominated by the seven-storey high image of a suited politician that had been plastered up the side of one of the apartment blocks.

Sitting on the cracked, tiled veranda, sipping sludgy black coffee, I asked my grandmother about the identity of the smiling figure at the end of the road.

"What, the painting down the end of the road? That's Nebbi Berri."

"What, Nebbi Berri, the leader of the Amal party?"

"Yes, he was our neighbour. He used to live just over the back there," she said, pointing beyond the garden wall at one of the adjacent apartment blocks.

I was a little stunned to discover that Aunt Maggie had lived next to such controversial neighbours. In 1983 Berri's name became infamous in the West when his militia was wrongly accused of the US embassy suicide bombing.

The Amal came under the western media spotlight again in 1985 when it seized most of the TWA passengers being held hostage by the Islamic militant group, *Hezbollah*, aboard a jet at Beirut airport. The media flocked to Berri's office in Mazraa and set up camp outside Aunt Maggie's house, waiting for news of the hostages. The media had gathered up the road, reporting from 'Muslim West Beirut' outside the walls of a Christian garden!

"The Amal guards used to patrol around here at night with a torch," my grandmother continued, "they used to look after Maggie and if there was anything she needed she would send them to the shops and they'd get it for her. She used to send them up onto the roof to pick mulberry. They were very nice chaps, very sociable."

Early in the evening of Orthodox Palm Sunday, I was jolted by an explosion of car horns which had erupted in a nearby street. Outside a troop of percussionists brandishing tambourines and drums were gathered at the entrance of an apartment block adorned with vivid bunting and a picture of the Ka'ba at Mecca. Suddenly the musicians burst into action, providing accompaniment to a cacophony of car horns as a joyful *Hajj* returnee climbed from an old Mercedes. The assembled crowd clamoured to welcome him home from pilgrimage. Meanwhile a man was euphorically sacrificing a sheep on the pavement, cutting its throat in accordance with *Halal* custom. I was strangely elated by the joyful, if bloody, scene and ready to leave the celebrations when I noticed a straight red line which had been daubed on a nearby doorway. Stopping a passer-by I enquired: "Is this sheep's blood from the sacrifice?"

The man looked at me a little quizzically before replying, "No. This is apartment number one."

★ ★ ★ ★ ★

I had been planning to visit the renovated area of downtown Beirut for some time and my opportunity came when an architectural student from a Lebanese University offered to show me around.

"The Green Line between East and West Beirut ran right through here," Walid said as we surveyed the freshly made roads which lead to the new port. "On a certain day the militia from East Beirut would take most of the buildings, the next day the militia from the west would push them back. The whole town was destroyed in the war."

The places of worship were the only ruins not demolished by the builders after the war and the churches and mosques, peppered with bullet holes, still bore the marks of militia gun battles in the downtown area. Walid was pointing to a crop of scarred buildings which sat on the edge of the new town. "Look down there. Two mosques and two churches sitting right next to each other. Take a picture of that," he said with a note of irony in his voice.

We made our way to the streets of the re-constructed town, walking on smoothly cobbled pavements between the ornate facades of the beautifully renovated buildings. Completing our circular tour of the town centre, we headed off in Walid's car towards Beirut's glamorous sea front strip, known as the Raouche. Walid lamented the architectural atrocities which had been committed on the Raouche, pointing to the regulation-busting tower blocks whose penthouse owners had been told they would be able to enjoy a view of Cyprus from their living rooms. When I was told a single apartment cost up to US$3 million, I wondered if it may have been cheaper for Beirut's jetset to move Cyprus a little closer to Lebanon.

Ten minutes further along the south-bound road we trundled into a breeze block shanty town. It seemed an odd place for an architect to bring a visitor as the crumbling buildings were either half-collapsed or half-completed. "This is a *Shi'ite* refugee camp. These are the people who fled from the south when Israel invaded in 1978 — they are still here. When Israel attacked in 1996 I was distributing aid to more refugees who had fled from the south. Suddenly an Israeli attack helicopter appeared just 40 metres from the place where we were working. We could see the pilot and he could see us. We were just hoping that he wouldn't shoot."

Turning inland, we passed through more slums. Bumping along an increasingly uneven dirt track I saw chickens grazing on the garbage. The flock of grubby birds were feasting on a dinner of trash and drinking from pools of filthy rain water that festered in the pot holes.

"This whole area is called Beirut's misery belt," Walid informed me as we pulled onto the newly constructed highway which ran from the airport to the reconstructed heart of the city. Glistening on the other side of the road was the white facade of Beirut's magnificent gladiatorial-style stadium. Passing by the side of the ground I was mesmerised by the gleaming walls until Walid broke my day dream.

"Here are Sabra and Shatila." The words made me shiver. In front of us lay the two Palestinian refugee camps where nearly 1000 people were massacred by the Phalange militia during the Israeli occupation of West Beirut in 1982. Nobody knows the precise death toll as many of the corpses were buried by the time the murderers left. In 1985 the camps' population were pulverised by the shells and gunmen of the Amal militia in the devastating 'camp wars'.

The now familiar site of refugee poverty filled the windscreen — a sewerless breeze block shanty town, built several stories high to accommodate a spiralling population. Being strangers to the locals, Walid advised that we stay in the car. Although famous, the camps are not tourist attractions.

Walid began to explain one of the consequences of the redevelopment programme. "You see, this main road passes straight from the main terminal building to the downtown development. Visitors arriving in Beirut drive past all these camps and don't even know they are here." The highway began to climb, guiding us over the roof tops of another two shanty towns. Pointing down at the Mar Elias camp on the left, Walid added: "Even Lebanese people are unaware of their existence. Today some young Lebanese people don't even know that there are Palestinians in Lebanon."

It was Orthodox Good Friday and I was visiting the local church in search of the priest. It was a hive of activity. A team of florists were busily dressing a table with red and white carnations while children darted in and out of the church with various pieces of furniture. In the nave a group of men were rearranging the chairs like stage hands preparing the theatre for the afternoon matinee.

Each time I stepped into the church I was overwhelmed by the sense of space created by the wide, sky blue domed roof. Elaborate glass chandeliers hung from the ceiling on thick chains, creating a sense of antiquity which disguised the fact that the church was constructed in the 1960s. Arrangements of flowers and foliage brightened the pews, but it was the more permanent decorations which drew my attention. Around the walls, icons glittered with gold paint, depicting biblical scenes and events from the lives of Christian saints. Between the nave and the altar stood a formidable marble screen, (the icononostasis), itself covered with portraits of icons whose stern, austere faces somehow pulled my gaze into their wide, piercing eyes. The images were not merely decorations. To Orthodox Christians they hold special significance as an aid to prayer whilst also telling a story from a particular saint's life. Art historians have likened the style of the sacred art of the Orthodox church to that of ancient Egyptian death portraits, suggesting that the former developed from the latter in the first centuries of Christianity.

The carnation-clad table was now being carried into the church under the watchful gaze of the florists. I began to feel worried that my presence would hinder the delicate operation so I moved to the terrace. Outside a table of food had appeared, hinting that the task force would soon stop work for lunch. As they prepared to eat I felt increasingly like a gatecrasher and was about to abandon my hunt for Father Michael, when he strolled through the gate. "You will have a bite with us? Come and eat, I must bless the food."

The table was covered with all manner of vegetarian dishes, the absence of meat due to the observance of Lent during which many Orthodox follow a vegan diet.

"*Fatoush*?" enquired the lady who was standing over a basin of the rich leaf and bread salad. Before I had a chance to answer my plate was being passed to the other end of the table, collecting an assortment of homous, falafel and pastry creations *en route*.

Witnessing the elaborate preparations for an Easter service, I asked Father Michael whether the church had been able to function in the same manner during the war when the area had been under Muslim-led militia control.

"I came to this church in 1985 when it was a very tense period and many Christians were being kidnapped in the area. I continued to hold services, we had meetings, we had prayers and we used to ring the bell. Of course when there was shelling or fighting nobody was able to come because the security situation didn't allow anyone to be outside."

Expecting the priest to tell me that the church had been closed for the duration of the hostilities, his answer came as a surprise. I asked him why he thought it was possible for the Christians to continue worship in the area during the war.

"Maybe, because the people of the area here had very good ties with the Muslims. Those who wanted to leave, left, but the people who stayed, the internal fabric of society, had good relations with each other." Father Michael paused briefly before adding: "That doesn't mean that negative things didn't happen, there were people who were kidnapped and the militia tried to occupy the houses of some Christians, not simply because they were Christians, but because they didn't have anyone to protect them."

Our conversation had been carefully monitored by an ever-growing number of inquisitive children. As I was preparing to leave, the group invited me to attend the midnight service on Saturday. Clearly proud of their traditions, they told me it was a very beautiful service and urged me not to miss it.

I took their advice and headed off to the church before midnight the following day. My route was lit by the minaret of the Abd al-Nasser mosque which was glowing neon green, illuminated by a rather garish fluorescent strip lighting. I arrived a little late and was greeted by the sight of the massed congregation standing on the terrace outside the church. Squeezing through the gate, I took my place in the crowd as the assembled were wedged from the iron railings to the closed doors of the church. They were standing on the stairs, the benches and the flower pots, each holding a candle as they listened to the priest who had taken up a position on the steps. Meanwhile the mighty church bell was providing a fierce accompaniment to the reading as a group of local strongmen jostled for the honour of ringing it. On the stroke of midnight the priest hammered on the church door three times before it mysteriously swung open. The congregation poured into the nave where the glass chandeliers had been set in motion, swinging back and forth as the service began and the thurible bearer sprinkled the whole building with the rich odour of incense.

The service finished in the early hours of the morning with the congregation wishing one another 'Happy Easter' and uttering the tidings I first heard a week earlier in the mountain village of Ghazir. "Joyeaux Pacques, Joyeaux Pacques." Tolling with all their might, the bell ringers jubilantly set about their task once again as the distant sound of the Muslim call to prayer drifted across the roof tops.

Walking the Valley of Death

by Chris Bradley

Unused to sitting on hard ground for such long periods, I shifted my feet and inadvertently knocked over the Kalashnikov that was resting against the wheel of a truck. A wild-looking Bedouin caught it in mid-fall so that I was literally staring down the gun barrel. He smiled a gold toothy grin and lay the gun across his lap. The barrel now pointed at my wedding tackle.

In a land full of surprises it was still surreal to find myself sitting under a blue tarpaulin, stretched between two trucks, and surrounded by a hundred of the most lawless, well-armed tribesmen in the Wadi Hadramaut of southern Yemen.

My journey had started 12 days and 300 walking kilometres earlier at the derelict trading town of Henin, where the sweeping sand dunes of the Rub al-Khali (the Arabian Empty Quarter) are funnelled into the eight kilometre wide entrance to Wadi Hadramaut. Every 60 or 70 years the rainstorms are catastrophic enough to push a huge wall of water down this valley to the Indian Ocean some 500 kilometres away. For the rest of the time this dry river valley, or *wadi*, is a public thoroughfare. Thousands of years ago it was used to transport frankincense and myrrh from the Dhofar region to Shabwa, Marib and onwards to the bustling markets of Petra, Gaza, Ancient Egypt, Greece and Rome. Those old merchants became wealthy, as did the towns that provided food, water and safety. Safety from the Bedouin tribes who attacked, plundered and murdered and amongst whose descendants I now sat.

My plan was simple. To walk solo and unsupported along the full length of Wadi Hadramaut — a name meaning 'Valley of Death'. To make it, I needed the generosity of the same Bedouin who were often more used to helping people disappear (albeit temporarily) and providing hospitality in a somewhat restricted environment — often referred to as kidnapping.

Three days into the trek I staggered, exhausted, into the walled trading city of Shibam and its eight-storey mud-houses. I was so shattered I could hardly lift my neck to look up at these 'skyscrapers of the desert'. My feet were blistered, my back felt half broken from the weight of my rucksack and my initial enthusiasm in tatters. Convinced there was no way I could walk another three weeks like this, I dumped everything non-essential and, reinvigorated for the challenge ahead, strode boldly through Seiyun, Tarim and onto the great pilgrimage site of Qabr Hud in a week. If I was to conquer the Hadramaut, I needed to attack it mentally, as much as physically.

For the last three days various people had talked about a Bedouin wedding taking place soon. Among those was Ahmed, a villager who walked some of the way with me. He was a sharp-featured, fuzzy-haired trader from Sana (not to be confused with Sana'a, the capital in the northern mountains), a village with a rich history of men emigrating to work in East Africa. For hundreds of years Hadrami men who lived in the Valley of Death have escaped the interminable tribal conflicts and some of the harshest climate on earth to earn a living abroad. They controlled trade in the Red Sea and East African ports; fighters got respected positions in the private armies of the Nizams of Hyderabad and Gujurat; and property speculators and developers earned fortunes in Singapore and Batavia.

Ahmed was connected to the groom's family and was going to the wedding as a representative of his branch of the family tree. Dressed in a checked futah, a kind of wraparound man's skirt and topped by a western shirt, his wirery frame and flip-flops hurried easily through the rough terrain that was covered by a talcum-powder-thin layer of dust. His pace was quick, especially compared to my own lumbering progress in desert boots, trousers with pockets for each day of the week and a still bulging rucksack. He had never been overseas, but his father and brother worked for years in Dar as-Salaam and Zanzibar, his father even returning with a second, but younger and darker, wife. He knew of Reagan, Clinton and Thatcher, but didn't think they were too friendly.

It was Saturday morning when we arrived. The scene of 30-odd cars with little groups of chatting men looked more like a car boot sale than a wedding. I was discreetly told to keep my distance from the women's section, tucked into a vertical fold of the dramatic landscape. Initial suspicions of my purpose there slowly gave way to curiosity when they realised I did not have a vehicle, did not work for an oil company and had no obvious connection with the Government.

Outside the cool shade of the tarpaulin, the midday sun beat down relentlessly. Ahmed, who had taken me under his protective wing, was outside talking when raised voices suddenly turned into a scuffle and two men rushed at me brandishing machine guns and rifles. As in the rest of Yemen, with everyone so well armed it's a situation you eventually get used to. There comes a point during an extended journey when the travel-soaked brain doesn't interpret what the eyes see anymore, but just accepts it before moving on to the next stimulation.

My Arabic was good enough to know when I am being ordered about and I was marched off to a nearby four-wheel drive. A kidnap, I thought. The array of new and expensive vehicles was impressive. To the outsider such a display would indicate this to be a wedding between two wealthy families. One wonders how these semi-nomadic traders can afford a new US$50,000 vehicle. The easy answer is that they can't. If they want a gleaming new Land Cruiser they simply wait for one to drive past and relieve the driver of the keys. It's even better if it belongs to one of the Western-backed oil or gas companies working in the Hadramaut region, the benefits of which have yet to be passed onto the locals.

Any Western worker inside the car used to be left to walk back to civilisation with the unfortunate driver. Lately they too have been used as bargaining chips during negotiations with the Government for the promised, but never delivered, improvements in medical, educational and water facilities.

Kidnapping is nothing new to the Bedouins. Successful desert trade, controlled by the Bedouin for thousands of years, has relied on similar negotiations when passing through tribal lands. In exchange for paying tributes or taxes on the goods carried, a member of that tribe, theoretically acting as a guide, would effectively be taken hostage by the caravan and held until they had safely travelled through.

The code of the desert is paradoxical. On one hand, raids and bloody tribal feuds can last for centuries. Yet in such an inhospitable environment, often the only way to survive is to rely on the generosity of others. If a stranger, traveller or even an enemy turns up, the only response is to offer what you have, even if this might put your own welfare and survival at risk. Replace this code of hospitality with hostility and no human could possibly make the Rub al-Khali their home.

Unsure of what was happening I was driven across the *wadi* and away from the wedding camp. But no sooner had we started than we stopped at the base of the cliff. The two men scrambled up the scree slope to a narrow ledge waving their Kalashnikov rifles to indicate I should follow. Reluctantly I did so. To my surprise the men showed me dark red inscriptions painted on the wall of an overhang, well above the level of any floods. At last I could put a name to where I was.

My only information for this second half of my walk beyond Qabr Hud was the chapter in Harold Ingram's 'Arabia and the Isles' where he recounts a camel journey made by him and his wife Doreen in the 1930's. He wrote about spending the night beside some red 'Dragon's Blood' texts at a place his Bedouin guides named Sadh — meaning 'dam', testifying to ancient attempts at controlling the floods. No evidence of a dam survives, but his guides said the site still had special significance. I guessed this was why the wedding was being held here. I declined the offer of a ride and walked the 300 metres back to camp.

My starting point was Henin, where the Ingrams spent their first night in the *wadi*, as did a few other travellers 60 years ago. Having trekked across the *jol* from the coast at Mukalla, they stayed with the Sultan of Henin. From there they explored the main towns and sites of the wadi, but only the Ingrams ventured the full length. As I stood above the ruined palace at Henin I felt the caress of their warm ghosts and began to feel something powerful at work. I wondered what it was.

The wedding afternoon was a combination of praying, religious discussions, singing and shooting. The Imam looked every bit the part, grey beard, immaculate dress, deep booming voice and was obviously someone who commanded great respect. He led the group prayers and followed it with discussions which, from what I could gather, extolled the sanctity of marriage, the virtues of family life and the benefits of the new diff-lock on the Toyota GX pick-up.

Three times during the day the dark-skinned, roughly dressed men took their places in a large circle, two groups standing opposite each other with a bucket in the middle. For ten minutes one group of 20 men would sing a high-pitched chant, with the others responding until they took up the hypnotic rhythm before passing it back again. The purpose of the bucket? So non-singers could grab a drink to combat the heat.

Away to one side a team of men busily cooked mountains of rice and fresh camel meat in huge metal pots. Sweet bubbling tea was always on the go, as was thick husk coffee and sticky dates. There was even a small shop in the back of a pick-up truck, but the person doing the swiftest business was the guy selling bullets.

The first was a 'short course' competition, with an old playing card wedged onto the end of a stick about 10 metres away. Each man with a gun — i.e. everybody — took it in turns to kneel down and fire at the card. The crack of gunfire was deafening, but not one of them missed the target, which eventually hung in tatters. It used to be the six of hearts.

The second was much more spectacular as they aimed at a small shaded area high up on the valley wall, about 200 metres across the *wadi* bed. The 'ppffuts' of bullets hitting scree were never more than a metre apart. I kept asking what they were firing at, but remained none the wiser. Any notions I had about the tribes using antiquated firearms that couldn't hit a barn door were quickly dispelled. These were serious marksmen. Then the inevitable happened. Ahmed thrust his rifle into my arms, saying in Arabic, "You're a man, you shoot".

I'd never fired a gun before and the first thing that struck me was how heavy it would be to drag around the desert. Cleverly, he had emptied the bullets from the magazine clip so that if I did turn out to be a madman (which many of them openly thought) I wouldn't shoot too many people.

A hush fell over the crowd as I knelt down and took aim, still unsure of exactly what I was shooting at. The noise of the shot cracked through my eardrums and the recoil twisted my shoulder uncomfortably. This was not funfair shooting. We all looked for the explosion of sand. A few murmurs started and I wondered why my bullet was taking so long to arrive. Alas there was no 'ppffut' and I still have no idea where the bullet ended up. The disappointed crowd was equally mystified and quietly disbanded. I hoped I hadn't shattered their impressions of great British desert explorers and warriors such as Lawrence and Thesiger.

By late afternoon more and more people had drifted into camp until there was more than 200, some of whom I recognised from earlier days on my trek, milling around. After the important sunset prayers we settled down for the great wedding feast of meat and rice, with everyone fingering the choicest camel chunks before passing them onto my plate. As the last rays of daylight dipped below the massive natural walls, a huge bonfire grew from the embers of the cooking fire, casting massive ogre-like shadows across the *wadi*. There was more singing and dancing and I could hear women's voices somewhere in the eerie darkness. But the best of this extraordinary day was still to come.

An hour after evening prayers and amid much shouting and frantic revving, several vehicles headed out of camp and down the wadi. Half-an-hour later I could just make out the faint echo of gunshots and see distant headlights pointing this way and that. Ahmed told me this tradition was where the groom took his new bride from her village and brought her to live with his family.

I clambered up the nearest scree slope to get a better view. A hazy kilometre away, six vehicles with blazing headlights, flashing orange hazards and honking horns were picking their way along the dusty track. From open windows and the backs of pick-ups single shots rang out. This time the bullets flight were not lost to the eye. Like tracer bullets racing across the black sky, the fiery arcs of yellow and green flashed above our heads, dying a kilometre behind us. Those at the camp answering by firing red and blue streaks over the heads of the oncoming carnival. A volley of deafening shots from a machine gun fired wildly upwards in multi-coloured spirals, only to die by the time the crumpled echo had rebounded from side to side in our sunken playground. If anyone stumbled upon us they could easily have thought a full-scale battle was in progress. The vehicles arrived in wild celebration, choking dust and of course, more shots.

Sleeping in the open that night, surrounded by lawless tribesman and the intermittent sound of gunfire, I realised there was something very special about the Hadramaut and there was no place on earth I would rather be.

Before sunrise, but well after early morning prayers and more religious discussions, I politely declined offers of a ride from those going to the coast as we sipped morning tea. I bade farewell to my hosts and started walking again.

Until now I didn't know whether it was possible to cross a 70 kilometre, waterless stretch of desert "without village or well" as Ignoramus had written. From the fairly useless Air Pillage Chart it looked as though the *wadi* broke up and there was no obvious route through. The wedding guests I had spoken to were adamant that I should not to go beyond a small village called Nisum. They said I would not be able to carry enough water to survive the walk to the next village and that I should get a lift or hire a camel.

With their words of advice in mind I set off down the dry river valley. You would think it would be impossible to get lost walking along a dry river bed, but on this day it seemed too easy. When another *wadi* enters as a tributary you just continue downhill. But even from my starting point I was only 660 metres above sea level. With a downhill gradient of about 1:800 the slope is impossible to detect, especially with jumbled rocks and dusty scrub scattered about the *wadi* bed. Add violent 90 degree bends in the main route and the fact that some of the *wadis* coming in are much larger, and it becomes very difficult, especially when faced with dwindling water supplies and extreme temperatures.

At one point I'd drunk 15 litres of water and was dipping into my permanent five litre reserve. Allowed an unlimited amount of water I would happily have walked right through the heat of the day, but to reduce my intake I rested in the shade to make noodles and tea between 10.30am and 2.30pm, which still gave me about eight walking hours per day. This was more than enough.

An hour before sunset I staggered into a shop-cum-grain-store-cum-infested rat hole in one of the sad looking collection of five huts called Nisum. The locals seemed somewhat bemused.

"Jamal?" They thought over the word and looked at each other.

"You want to hire a Jamal?"

I nodded.

"Haven't seen Jamals around here for ages," one eventually grunted.

I was contemplating my choices when the final vehicle from the wedding trundled into sight, it's axles bottoming out and almost bending under the weight. It was the mobile shopkeeper seeing what he could unload at Nisum before making the 70 km crossing. I had five minutes to decide. Get a lift and check the route to see whether I could walk it; organise water dumps; hire a camel at the other end or stay here until a camel turned up. I opted for the former.

Not counting the 15 minute stop for sunset prayers, it took exactly 100 minutes to get to an even sadder collection of two huts called Hint. Despite being an incredibly uncomfortable ride with 10 people, two goats, no deodorant and all covered in layers of dust in the back of a suspension-dead pick-up, I calculated we averaged around 30mph, which would make it approximately 80 kms.

Shumayl Salem was another hitch-hiker only too glad to get off the overcrowded dune buggy. He lived in Hint. In fact he and his family were Hint. He had not been at the wedding but was lucky enough to get a lift whilst walking back from Sana after collecting some medicine for his sick daughter — a journey of four days!

Through the evening we negotiated a non-riding rate for the hire of his camel and minder Hamid, sealing the deal with another fine meal of fish and rice cooked by his wife. I went through the motions of inspecting the camel as Salem asked, but in the pitch darkness I really had no idea what I was looking for, other than checking that there was a leg at each corner. I settled down for the night on the roof of his animal shed and I'm sure I heard the goats move away around 3am — probably because of my smell. As I looked at the stars above the *wadi's* great walls I felt disappointment at breaking the purity of my walk with a lift. But I was about to serve my penance by re-walking that water-less section, not once but twice.

As dawn began to break, 15-year-old Hamid filled an old truck inner tube with water (35 litres I reckoned) and strapped it to one side of the camel, using my rucksack on the other as a counterbalance. This was how it was supposed to be — no worries about water and no heavy straps digging into my shoulders. With Hamid leading the camel, I could now investigate all those things that were usually too much trouble — grand vistas from high up the *wadi* wall and areas of dried mud, mosaics of crazy paving that cracked like plates of corn flakes under my rapidly deteriorating boots.

We only walked for five hours that day, but covered much more than I ever could alone. As Hamid found a suitable place to let the camel graze, I set about my task of starting a fire and making tea. Looking directly west down the rose-red *wadi*, the huge sun filled the sky as if all the towns and villages I had passed through were on fire.

Hamid sat back enthralled as I unpacked. Throughout the day he had hardly said a word, unless asked a question. I tried to bring him into my journey by showing him the map and naming the towns I had already walked through.

Nothing.

I showed him the compass and how the head torch swivelled on and off.

Still nothing.

As a last effort I offered him a slug of Dioralite. You can guess his reaction. He wrapped himself up in the camel's blanket and fell soundly asleep. My own sleep was fitful and disturbed. Maybe I was getting too used to carrying the rucksack?

Up and off by 5.30am, Hamid reluctantly accepted half a biscuit for breakfast on the hoof. Six hard hours later we drifted into Nisum. The same old men were sitting around the 'shop'. I imagined their conversation.

"Oh my God, here's that crazy Farangi again."

"But look, he's got a camel."

"So why did he want a camel from us?"

"And why is he coming in from the direction he wanted to go?"

I greeted them politely, bought Hamid and myself some warm Pepsi, bade them farewell and started walking back from where we had come. By now, Hamid was completely confused.

Another one-and-a-half days walking brought Hamid and I sweatily back into Hint late on the afternoon of Day 16. Altogether we had walked 140 kilometres in 21 hours. That night, lying once again on the animal shed I knew my goal was achievable. I slept well, contentedly cocooned in the protective walls of the 'Valley of Death'. All that remained was a simple 120 kilometre stroll down to the coast.

If anything, the *wadi* became even more impressive and in some places the sandstone was interrupted by volcanic outcrops. Each day I passed a few walking locals and the occasional pick-up trundled between decrepit villages. I passed into the governorate of al-Mahra, where the mood of these new people changed as dramatically as the scenery. They were less open, more confined and secretive. Certainly less friendly. Now beyond the dry section, I was dealing with people who inhabited the wadi from the coast. These were not the Bedouin of the desert. They were from seafaring stock, now tied down as peasant farmers. They eyed me with suspicion and provided little warmth.

Towards the coast the landscape opened up with long quiet days in spectacular, untouched canyon scenery. My final link with the desert was the fortress on the giant volcanic outcrop of Husn *Ad*, an early control point for the ancient traders wishing to enter the Hadramaut from the coast. Lost in the swirling desert sands are the stories of the Ad tribe, the original inhabitants of Hadramaut. A race of giants, everything about the legend of the *Ad* people is huge — graves up to 30m in length and according to the Book of Genesis, men with life-spans of 1200 years, 1000 wives and 4000 children.

The mid-point of my journey had been the ancient pilgrimage site of Qabr Hub, the tomb of the Ad tribe prophet Nabi Allah Hud, whose story was later incorporated into the Qur'an. Thought also to be Eber in The Bible, his huge grave may be the resting site of the great-great-grandson of Noah, and the father of Qahtan, from whom all true Arabs — the Qahtanids — are said to descend.

As Harold Ingrams wrote: "In the beginning, God created the Heaven and the Earth. Here it seemed that creation had stopped at the very beginning. You cannot help it, in the Hadramaut, you are living in Genesis." There is something very powerful about the Hadramaut. But I don't know what it is.

Even to this day, I'm not sure if I was ever introduced to the groom. I certainly didn't meet the bride.

Escape from Butterfly Valley

by Steve Davey

"Turkey an Arab country? Naw!" replied an Australian backpacker who had spent the previous week sporting little more than a slightly lop-sided goatee and a Balinese sarong — in the days before David Beckham, out on the town with Posh Spice, had made such a garment irredeemably unfashionable.

So far his experience of Turkey had been 10 days in the travellers' hideaway of Butterfly Valley, near the tourist resort of Olu Deniz. He couldn't understand why, when asking for a cup of coffee on the mainland, he was given a miniature glass of sweet dark brown liquid and not a cup of Nescafé like he was used to.

I had tried to explain, but even the travel-writers' cliches of 'Gateway to the East', 'Ottoman Empire' and 'Arab Hospitality' failed to register. All he wanted to know about was ANZAC Day at Gallipoli and tree-houses on the Adriatic Coast.

At Butterfly Valley everyone referred to the rest of Turkey as "The Mainland", even though it wasn't an island. In fact it was a cove, virtually cut off from the outside world, only reachable by a chugging, lurching and leaking motor boat of the 'How many people does this take?', 'How many do you have?' variety.

I went to the Valley purely to meet a New Zealand friend who, having exhausted all efforts to stay in the UK except marriage or death, was hitting some of the latest trendy traveller destinations in a swansong before heading home to a small town on the other side of the world. Judging by the conversation we had on the phone I was also coming to rescue him from terminal hippiedom.

"Oh Man, you've got to come out, this place is beautiful, lounging on the beach all day, it's like a commune, cut off from the outside world and man, we'll stay in a tree house. And the chicks…" Apart from that, I needed a holiday. So with the excuse to myself and the taxman that I was researching traveller culture in Turkey, I caught the next cheap and cheerful charter flight from London's Gatwick Airport.

After a horrendously cramped flight I survived the scrum to get to the head of the queue at Dalaman Airport so I could part with £10 for the privilege of getting a little brown postage stamp stuck in my passport and share a nightmare three-hour taxi ride to Olu Deniz with three other travellers. The driver reached psychopathic speeds. I knew I was back in Asia when he adopted the standard habit of switching off the headlights as soon as we left the town's street lights behind, no doubt in order to gain that extra little bit of fuel efficiency, albeit at the risk of killing us all.

We were all dumped on the beach at Olu Deniz at about 5am. There was nothing to do except sit around and wait, them for the guesthouses to open and me for breakfast and the 10am boat to Butterfly Valley. Occasionally swigging from a duty-free bottle of vodka, I could already feel the gulf between Butterfly Valley and the real world opening up.

After a bilious boat ride where the water lapped worryingly close to the side of the boat and the other passengers — all backpackers — lounged around with assumed poses of studied nonchalance, we rounded a headland. The cove was beautiful, with a pebble beach curving around azure blue water. Towering cliffs on either side reached out into the water, meeting a couple of kilometres behind the beach. About 20 people lazed on the beach and more appeared from the scrub which separated the shore from a large restaurant. To the right there appeared to be a large, unfinished two storey house, missing both walls and roof. To my left, clinging halfway up a cliff and about 50 feet out to sea from the beach was a ledge which appeared to house a bar. More heads appeared to watch our arrival. I couldn't see any butterflies or tree-houses, but it didn't dampen my enthusiasm. The place looked perfect.

My friend, who I'll call Tony because his real name is Blair, waded waist-deep into the water to meet the boat, a beautiful smile on his face. I handed over the vodka and jumped over the side to wade back in with him. To worry about getting wet at a 'Captain-Cook-Discovers-the-New-World' moment like this would have been churlish.

On the beach more travellers had materialised to help unload the boat. Without a word they formed a perfect chain from waist deep next to the bobbing boat, all the way to the restaurant. Boxes, sacks of food and crates of beer were all passed from hand to hand, as were the newcomers' bags. If they had not scrambled over the side to join in, the newcomers would probably have been passed up as well. More and more people ran down to join the line until it was so crowded there were too many people making it all but impossible to pass stuff along. As soon as one person turned round to pass a box to the next it bumped into their chest, causing them to step back, knocking into the person in front of them and so on. The atmosphere was like a cross between Woodstock and an American collegiate outward bound course. That should have been my first warning. But, oblivious to it all, I strolled up to the reception chatting idly with Tony. My second warning should have come when they explained the rules. To stay one night cost so much; breakfast, lunch and dinner each had their own price on top and colour-coded tickets, or you could buy the lot at a small discount. Since there was nowhere else to eat, the only people who didn't benefit from that deal were anorexics or escapees, so I dutifully shelled out for the full board option and — assured that I had a place reserved in a tree house — sauntered off to the Cliff Bar.

I had a very uneasy feeling, but the first few vodkas put a stop to that and I felt warm with renewed enthusiasm. I tried to like Butterfly Valley, I really did, but looking around from the vantage point of the Cliff Bar with an air of cynical detachment I had a sneaking suspicion that life was not as wonderful as it seemed. I could see through this idyll of peace and tranquility. This was nothing more than a Butlins holiday camp for travellers, with a leaning towards the tie-dye. A hippyesque retreat for whom Goa was too far, or too expensive or too adventurous. A place where juggling or bongo playing were regarded as important life skills.

In short, the place was too easy. There was no elbowing your way through *souks*, sitting at pavement cafes waiting for a souvelaki and sipping Turkish coffee whilst puffing on a water-pipe. There were no ruins of great empires and civilisations. Instead, the place ran on a full board system — three tickets for food and one for a bed. A sanitised version of the East. A Turkey for those who don't like things too Turkish.

The realisation hit home with a vengeance, but at least I had my bed to look forward to. For most of my childhood and a large part of my adult life I had always dreamt of tree houses. Whether it be the result of too many Tarzan films or just a Boys Own imagination I don't know, but I always wanted, nay coveted a tree house of my own. I can remember one autumn my parents came home with a weedy sapling to plant in the back garden. In my mind I was already planning the tree house I would build the following year. It turned out to be an almond tree that was useless for anything — including almonds. It died 10 years later without ever producing an edible almond or holding so much as a bird box — let alone a prepubescent's dream tree house.

Needless to say when I finally lurched off to find my reserved spot in the tree house I was bitterly disappointed. My backpack lay in the corner of the unfinished building I had seen from the boat. Not even the upper storey — my tree house was seven-and-a-half inches off the ground. I was gutted.

I don't know where the Turkish tree house thing came from, maybe some enterprising carpenter built a genuine tree house somewhere and rented it out to some passing tourists. Before long everyone wanted to stay in one and it became the thing to do. Supply must have outstripped demand and soon people were happier to stay in an 'almost' tree-house. After a while — probably as the result of shockingly lax Turkish Trade Descriptions legislation — tree-house transmuted itself to mean any house made of trees. And still we lapped it up.

Despite my initial disappointment and reservations, life at Butterfly Valley soon settled in to pleasant monotony. We were usually woken in our *al fresco* sleeping quarters by sunrise, although tended to lie in until the kitchen staff — those sad travellers whose financial position meant that they would do anything to stretch out their money and time before returning to the real world — had prepared breakfast.

Then with varying degrees of hangover and intestinal uncertainty, we would lurch off to the optimistically titled 'restaurant' for a mixture of eggs, ham, bread, jam and watery coffee.

This barely edible hurdle surpassed, we would all head to the beach and lounge around in the sun, or prompted by an Australian called Darren, try our hand at floating. Floating — even in the sea — is not as easy as it appears. Darren was an expert. Not only did he have the right body mass ratio, he had technique, style even. Most of us could manage the sprawling star-float, arms and legs splayed, deep breath with shallow breathing on top of that to keep from sinking or suffocating. Darren had perfected the 'Lotus Float', which suprisingly enough involved floating in the Lotus position. It says a lot about Butterfly Valley that we were impressed by his technique and considered it something to aspire to. When he was not floating, Darren would sit in the Cliff Bar and read 'Zen and the Art of Motorcycle Maintenance' until it was time to plod down to the kitchen to take his hand in ruining whatever meal was on offer. Darren was a long-timer and I secretly felt he had been in the Valley too long.

About an hour before lunch tour boats from the mainland would loom on the horizon like marauding Roman galleys, and we would all scramble up to the Cliff Bar and sprawl on fake Ottoman style cushions, drink beer and look disdainfully as the boats moored just off shore and disgorged their fat, pink cargoes. When it was time for lunch we would troop down and file across the beach to queue for whatever slop Darren and his colleagues had made for us. Then it was back to the bar until the last boat left, and woe betide any visitor who came up to our hideaway. They were generally glared at and made to feel uncomfortable until they finished their drinks and left.

They were, after all, only tourists — lounging around on beaches and staying in hotels with breakfast, dinner and sometimes even lunch provided. We were different: we were travellers. The irony and hypocrisy of this escaped us as we waved our colour coded tickets for three meals a day and slept in tree-houses which were just two storey flop pads with the roof missing. That didn't matter. They were called tree-houses which meant we could legitimately write in our diaries — sorry 'Journals', only tourists and love-lorn school girls keep diaries — that we stayed in a tree-house on the Adriatic coast.

The only person who welcomed the tour boat was a Canadian we called Jesus, mainly because he bore a remarkable resemblance to... well Jesus. As soon as the first boat appeared Jesus would plunge into the water and swim out to meet it. This was all part of his act as they would reach the beach in a few minutes anyway. He would haul himself up onto the deck and juggle for money for a few minutes and then swim to the next boat. Bloated tourists with lobster-pink bellies hanging over unsightly skimpy bathers would use up unwarranted amounts of VHS on him. When each tired of the other, he would rejoin us at the Cliff Bar and smugly count his money smugly — and he never bought a round. God we hated him!

Although I had not read it at the time, life at Butterfly Valley was like everyone trying to recreate Alex Garland's 'The Beach', only without the crap 'Bobby-Ewing-woke-up-in-the-shower' style ending. Unfortunately, like most aspiring egalitarian Utopian societies it was largely devoid of fun, especially lacking the over-the-top hedonism I look forward to on a holiday. Over the years travellers seem to have got more serious and more responsible. Butterfly Valley reflected this change.

Unlike 'The Beach' there was no dope. There were rumours — a delivery next week, a few plants growing at the end of the valley or mushrooms in the shadow of the cliffs — but nothing ever materialised and despite all of the fuss and moaning, no one seemed to care. We just sat round, drank beer and had the occasional session on Turkish *Raki*. The hungry glances which greeted my bottle of vodka should have been a clue as to the deprivations and disappointments to follow.

People also seemed to be far more moral than I remember travellers being. There was little or no sleeping around. Everyone was either travelling as a couple, had a partner back home and was being faithful to them, or had just split up with a partner back home and were too emotionally disturbed for 'that-kind-of-thing.' Topless sunbathing was frowned upon, and when a French couple turned up, tuned in and dropped out by sunbathing nude the disapproval was so palpable even they felt it and covered up. Most people seemed to be *en route* from sixth form to University rather than any more exotic locations. And the conversations!

They all seemed to be about money or hardship — as little as possible of the former and as much as possible of the latter. In our rigid set of values it was perfectly okay to spend any amount of money on alcohol or carpets, but spend one penny more than the absolute minimum on travel or accommodation and you were derided. It was as though, to try and put some purpose into our empty meanderings on this planet, we had opted to live monastic lives. What happened to a little bit of luxury?

We would sit around the Cliff Bar for hours, mutually reminiscing about various countries we had visited — ostensibly friendly, but with an undercurrent of veiled competition. Sparring, just looking for an opening, a weakness. When two people had been to the same place the battle begun.

"So, where did you stay?" Keep that poker-face. Were they bluffing? You mutter a reply — stupidly this was the one time on the trip where after 36 hours on a bouncing local bus driven by a suicidal 14-year-old you treated yourself to a relatively nice room costing all of US$2 to recover. They gleefully trump you; "I stayed at a place called 'The Shitpit' — no water, toilet was a leaky bucket in the corner and I managed to get a damp bed in a 30-person dormitory for the equivalent of 20 cents!"

Your feeble excuse is brushed aside: "Only 36 hours, you must have got the VIP Tourist bus. Ours took four days and broke down seven times. My girlfriend died of exposure and I was still up at 5:30am the next day to crawl over broken glass for 20 miles on the pilgrimage circuit like the locals do!" Or some such drivel.

'Like the locals' was our mantra. We would recount stories of great exploits — crossing deserts or scaling mountains to visit remote villages in an effort to get to the locals. "I travelled for four days on a donkey with no food or water to get to this village, but it was great — THERE WERE NO TOURISTS!".

I resisted pointing out that the delightfully collectively titled 'locals' probably didn't buy into the great traveller/tourist debate, preferring that we all left them alone and that being confronted by a traveller full of 'respect' but no understanding was probably as much of an intrusion as a coach-party of octogenarian Americans with external plumbing. At least the tour group would spend more and not mercilessly haggle for the 'local prices' contained in a three-year-old Lonely Planet.

I remember a cycle-rickshaw wallah at Agra in India and his assertion that travellers were just 'beggar tourists'. We might all look on ourselves as travellers — adventurers on life's highway, but in many countries of the world we are just scruffy tourists who don't like spending money and who argue over the smallest amount. 'Respect' might figure highly in our currency, but it doesn't put food on the table or provide medicine for the children.

I even resisted asking that if the 'locals' were so great then why were we all sitting in Butterfly Valley where there were none! Well, there were a few. They ran the place and collected the money, but try as I might I can't remember any of them. They blended into the background — more European hoteliers than Arab hosts.

Our other great hang-up was time. You weren't a proper traveller unless you were going to be away for at least a year. Shorter trips — no matter how adventurous — just didn't cut it and were looked on as tourist stuff. "What, you mean that you are only away for a month and have friends, family, a job and a life back home — you tourist!" There would always be some dysfunctional who was away for years — normally a weird, friendless soul, probably on the run from their home country and ostracised by family and friends. But to us they would be a messiah.

One morning I couldn't take it any more. After a particularly colourless breakfast which had by now reduced most of us to a state of intestinal catastrophe I struck.

"Let's get out of here today mate, this place is doing my head in. I can even hear bongos in my sleep!"

"Naw, let's give it a few more days — just chill."

Chill — the universal travellers trump card. Chill — the competitive put down meant to indicate that the speaker is in some way more relaxed and 'travellery' than you.

"That bastard has stolen my wallet/charged me $10 for a coke/spat in my face!"

"Chill out man, be cool!"

Just wait until it happens to you and we'll see how chilled you are.

As a compromise we decided to do the next best thing to leaving The Valley: a group of us would climb the cliffs at the back to reach the fabled restaurant at the top. This was the restaurant at the end of our universe and held a mystical status at Butterfly Valley.

It lay on the outskirts of a small village at the top of the soaring cliffs which cut us off from the outside world. A steep and dangerous path led up the almost vertical cliff face, and in some places you had to haul yourself up with the aid of knotted and rotten ropes — thoughtfully left there by some long forgotten villager. Tales abounded in the Valley of people who had not made it back (although I tend to think that once they reached the outside world they got a bus out of the area, preferring to leave everything behind than be sucked back into the vacuum of the Valley). Another story involved two unfortunate travellers who tried to find an alternative route down and became stuck on a ledge halfway down, nearly perishing of hunger and exposure until some locals heard their now feeble cries for help and led them to safety.

It was with an appropriate sense of gravity that we made our preparations and headed off, completely forgetting to bring any water, for the hike to the foot of the cliffs.

We soon reached the towering walls at the back of the valley, although still without seeing a single butterfly. An unmarked trail led steeply upwards and we began to climb, nervously joking about what lay in store. Soon we were all sweating and out of breath. We had, of course, left the climb until the late afternoon when the sun was at its hottest. With insults now familiar relationship to injury, I managed to split my pants while climbing up the first rocky scree. At least I was cooler, although I'm sure those behind me did not appreciate their enhanced view.

When we reached the first rope climb I nearly turned back. A knotted and frayed rope lay beguilingly on a 40 foot rock face that sloped at an angle of at least 70 degrees. Not the worlds greatest obstacle, but the couple of hundred foot drop to the bottom just a meagre few inches from the path where we now stood, meant the consequences of any slip would be fatal. None of us had the guts to turn back, so to my great relief we continued upwards. Not that I am any good with heights — I get nose-bleeds climbing a ladder — but nothing was going to make me to spend another night at Butterfly Valley.

At each new obstacle we would hesitate and carry on with even less enthusiasm and vigour — if that were at all possible. By now I was exhausted and could only think about how we would have to climb down the next morning.

After what seemed like an eternity, a couple of rope climbs and a few barely disguised moments of vertigo we arrived at the top. The cliffs gave out to a small house with a large extension set at the edge of the drop amongst small gnarled trees. The views were, admittedly, spectacular, but spoilt slightly by the fact they were of Butterfly Valley.

By now we were dirty and sweaty, and in my case with my arse hanging out of a great vent in my trousers, but the good people who owned the 'restaurant' (in reality a private house which served meals and allowed you to crash on the bare floor afterwards) seemed pleased to see us. We lounged around until the meal was ready, playing cards, drinking beer and making unpleasant comments about each others odour following the climb.

The meal was wonderful — although in the tradition of Butterfly Valley there was no choice, just a set menu divided amongst however many people had made it up the cliffs. After the Euro-camping style food we had endured below, this was a veritable feast. Real Turkish food cooked by real Turkish people.

After the meal we walked out to the top of the cliffs to look out to the horizon and stare at the flickering lights of the Butterfly Valley restaurant far below, trying to put off the dreaded moment when we would try to sleep on the hard concrete floor. We had climbed a good few hundred metres and the air felt cool and fresh. We sat around happy and content. Emboldened by my first Turkish meal after so many days in Turkey, and desperate to finally escape The Valley, I tried again.

"So mate, how about heading to Olympos tomorrow morning? There's a beach, loads of phosphorescence in the water, some ruins and we can even stay in a tree-house!"

Victory. I'm sure it was the tree-house that swung it.

The Daily Telegraph
adventure
Travel and Sports Show 2000

* Over 50 Free Travel Talks
* Features
* Over 200 Exhibitors
* Expedition Planning
* Worldwide Adventure Holidays
* Independent Travel Advice
* Travel Writing and Photography Seminars
* Job Opportunities Abroad
* Health Advice
* Flights
* Safaris
* Latest Equipment
* Special Offers and Competitions

14th-16th January 2000 Olympia, London

This is an annual event organised by: ATS Event Ltd. Tel: 01795 844400 Email: info@atsevents.com

supported by travel TV THAT TAKES YOU THERE

95·8 CAPITAL FM